THE DIFFICULTY OF CROSSING A FIELD

THE DIFFICULTY OF CROSSING A FIELD

NINE NEW PLAYS

Mac Wellman

Foreword by Helen Shaw

University of Minnesota Press
Minneapolis
London

Infrared was previously published by Samuel French, Inc.; copyright 2000 by Mac Wellman. *The Difficulty of Crossing a Field* was published in *Theater* (Yale) 27, no. 2 (May 1997). *Antigone* was published in *Theater* (Yale) 32, no. 2 (April 2002) and also appears in the author's book of poetry, *Miniature* (New York: Roof Books, 2002). Portions of *Bitter Bierce* were published in *Brooklyn Review,* no. 20 (2003). An early version of "Speculations: An Essay on the Theater" was published in *Theatre Forum,* no. 20 (2002). *Jennie Richee* was first published in *Play: A Journal of Plays,* no. 2: Puppetry (November 2004).

Published by the University of Minnesota Press
111 Third Avenue South, Suite 290
Minneapolis, MN 55401-2520
http://www.upress.umn.edu

Library of Congress Cataloging-in-Publication Data

Wellman, Mac.
The difficulty of crossing a field : nine new plays / Mac Wellman ; foreword by Helen Shaw.
p. cm.
ISBN 978-0-8166-5504-5 (hc : alk. paper) — ISBN 978-0-8166-5505-2 (pb : alk. paper)
I. Title.
PS3573.E468D5 2008
812'.54—dc22

2008025869

Printed in the United States of America on acid-free paper

15 14 13 12 11 10 09 08 10 9 8 7 6 5 4 3 2 1

Contents

FOREWORD

Mac Wellman and Things of the Devil

Helen Shaw

In *Q's Q*, a mischievous, behind-the-scenes lampoon à clef, a regional theater's artistic director meets a gruesome end. The chief suspect is, of course, a playwright. Driven insane by the endless development process (and already a little lupine around the edges), the poor writer gets hairier and scarier . . . until he changes into his true form. A werewolf. Readers, be alert. This is the closest Mac Wellman ever gets to autobiographical confessionalism.

While Wellman may walk among us disguised as a mild-mannered, bespectacled dramatist (even sporting, on occasion, a straw boater), his true self is as the wolf-in-professor's-clothing, always ready to rip the throat out of theater-homogenizing sheep. Despite his Obies and his NEA grants, Wellman is still the dangerous champion of anticonventionalism, running on a platform of theatrical change and linguistic subversion. On panels, he starts fights and then leans back with a twinkle. He refers to himself as a Damnable Scribbler. And his highest word of praise is *demented.* Since a 1984 essay, "The Theatre of Good Intentions," he has been the cynosure in a heaven full of experimental playwrights who rail against what Jonathan Lear, in his book *Open Minded,* called a "tyranny" of "the already known." Wellman and his group—like minds include John Jesurun, Len Jenkin, and Maria Irene Fornes—take issue with "issue" drama, the journalistic variety that simply declaims a foregone (Families are good! Abuse is sad!) conclusion. "Geezer theatre," as he christens it, aims at worst for coziness and at best for guilt—since a guilt-struck audience can (cozily) reassure itself that it has "learned" something.

For writers who recognize their art form as anarchic, protean, and strange, this topical realism represents theater's living death. Wellman's term for the avant-garde's reactive strategy is "affective fantasy," the unfolding of dreamlike scenarios that bubble with meaning but never announce it. Stylistically, the movement away from pseudopsychological, sentimental, family dramas has happened—despite what the theaters in our neighborhoods may still be programming. The theatrical front has long since moved decisively on to the Modernist Project, in which the artist interrogates the medium before the message. Only in the world of the Pulitzer committee has the form stagnated. In some ways it's exhausting to still be repeating admonitions by Witkacy, by Artaud, by Tristan Tzara. Didn't Gertrude Stein fight this battle already? Didn't John Cage?

The wider world of theater, the parts outside the shrinking downtown Shangri-La, may yet be resistant because when people think of the avant-garde, they think of difficulty. It is surely hard work mining meaning from embedded prose. When the invocation in *The Invention of Tragedy* continues (after "a pause of inappropriate dogginess") with "O mighty minimax whereby of the full flower all rings doth make the pseudocrocodile arise and knuckled be and thus left to lift all shoes to an an o pied piper of care," the uninitiated might just tuck their tails and skulk away. In fact, this bizarre operetta about a cat who refuses to belong washes over us like "real" opera, in which non-Italian speakers can slowly learn fragments of the language thanks to repetition and choral insistence. (Afterwards you may have trouble remembering that cats have tails rather than *chails.*) Because of his diabolical language games, Wellman sometimes gets the unfair reputation of being obscure, nonlinear, highfalutin. In fact, many Wellman plays are practically vaudeville. His heroines are feisty young women who are handy with weapons (*Jennie Richee*) or snappy comebacks (the pugnacious girl in *Psychology*); his setups come from science fiction or noir. He tells anyone who'll listen that he got into theater because it's "a low, sleazy, discredited art form that had to do with sex and things of the devil," and the work has never shed a certain cheerful, disreputable flavor since.

Ever since Godot, serious playwriting has been about how to describe absence, and so Wellman's work is sometimes best described by what isn't there. In *Antigone,* Wellman wants to hew to a tragic line, but tragedy needs something immense in order to fracture it. What "truth" could be as dominant as Sophocles' gods? In the original, Creon and Antigone are pincered between a religious and a social certainty, neither of which can give way. In a post-Nietzschean world, Wellman casts about for something similarly solid, landing on that old bedrock, cause and effect. Things happen out of order; deaths repeat. With the Shriek Operator, played in the Big Dance production by demented Santa Claus Leroy Logan crooning into his microphone and deflating causal certainties, the murdered certainty was logic. In *The Fez,* on the other hand, the absence is the play itself. Like a John Cage composition, it exists merely as a list of directions to put on a play. Clearly, a ritual must be performed, but in the absence of an idol, the reader is left to invent one. In Jim Findlay's stage design for the opera *The Difficulty of Crossing a Field,* the stage was built around a giant, square well, so that it was the stage that was absent. It's no wonder Wellman was drawn to Ambrose Bierce's protagonist—who, you'll notice, doesn't exist. Count how many times he has important things crawl out of or into holes (*Infrared* actually has a hole as a speaking character). Clearly, he means to leave plenty of spare lacunae lying around, just in case some unexpected guest (or meaning) needs to clamber in and join us.

Mentally as well as linguistically, Wellman cannot resist a pun. In *Bitter Bierce,* his almost documentary approach to theatrical biography, he lobs Ambrose Bierce's best bons mots at us at speed. Sometimes the puns ("The heavy end of the match is the light end") pun from English into English; sometimes they swing off into a new language of their own. In the grinding mill of his brain, "If the shoe fits" becomes scene 31 of *A Morphology of Small Errors:* "Go, foo of shits, thy sway." He even puns in other languages, or permits the many translations of a word—in *Antigone,* he repeats the famous Sophoclean chorus so that man is at once "incredible" and "weird." Despite the dark workings of his mind, the images he works in are whole, hale ones of geodes and geese and fezzes and other things you'll find in a halfway decent small town parade. Things aren't broken or decaying—no Heiner Müller abattoirs or dusty Beckettian attics—they either exist, or they vanish neatly down one of his oeuvre's many holes. He has been to the deconstructionists' mountaintop; he has read the very choppy tablets given down by the Black Mountain gang and the Language Poets (he is one). But he also returns to us with their message. Rather than doodling off into archer and stranger territories, he somehow takes his fragmented language and splices it back into something irrefutably dramatic.

Since the staggering success of his Crowtet, the sequence that encompasses *A Murder of Crows, The Hyacinth Macaw, Second-Hand Smoke,* and *The Lesser Magoo,* Wellman has been our true American Gothic, capable of painting strange, poetic landscapes full of everyday objects. He changed tacks for Steinian language junkets like *Terminal Hip,* which threw caution and meaning to the winds, and sailed straight for linear satires like the prude-poking *7 Blowjobs.* Prolific and tricksy, he skitters away from a style when he feels himself hardening into mannerism. This decade's work—from 1997 to 2007—betrays that same fluidity, although he seems to be dicing finer and spreading wider. In these nine plays, you'll find fully nine different genres. In some cases, a collaborator calls the tune. Making a work for the multimedia, projection-heavy Ridge Theater, Wellman dreams up *Jennie Richee,* a palimpsest of outsider artist Henry Darger's work and his life. It's clear that images will bleed into one another and that he is writing for a flattened picture plane. *Antigone,* on the other hand, runs red with movement, since the Paul Lazar–Annie-B Parson–Big Dance Theater production needed, frankly, lots of dances. Now he seems to be listing increasingly toward opera—perhaps because he likes how David Lang's music for *The Difficulty of Crossing a Field* stays cool-headed enough to partner his syntax without swamping it.

So how do you read one? A Mac Wellman play, because it has so much to do with darkness, should heighten, metaphorically, your peripheral vision. Without the glare of a plotlight, you can sense his narratives moving around just out of sight, rather like the "small unpleasant animal" crawling around in his *Antigone.* Idea-wise, a wink is as good as a nod—not to mention a whole monologue belaboring the concept of yes. Themes will spring up and hover, never to be explained into submission. He suggests ideas rather than elaborates on them, which may explain why it's so hard to get bored in his plays, even when they are trying hard to beat you into a trance with repetition and chanting dwarves. He seeds his text with allegories but rarely harvests them. The soil is chock-full of Hegel and Wittgenstein and Steiner, but in MacLand, secrets stay buried.

Of course, it's important to remember that these scripts are only *representing* Wellman's work. A script is always just a two-dimensional map for a three-dimensional territory. In Wellman's case, a sense of stage space so drives his works (the way that *Psychology; or, Bring a Weasel and a Pint of Your Own Blood* works with stacked playing spaces, or how *The Invention of Tragedy* thinks about the wings) that they don't quite exist until they are in production. Wellman has an enormous affection and interest in the mechanics and collaborations of theater—never, sad to say, a foregone conclusion for a playwright. His airy compositions (riddled with those holes) leave ample room for a director to maneuver. He also delights in nothing so much as causing other people trouble. With a simple stage direction (dancers must "do the Jamaican Car Service"), he knows he can throw one director, one stage manager, four designers, and a handful of actors into paroxysms of delicious dismay. Setting those puzzles for others to solve actually leads to what he thinks of as "accuracy." He notes that "when I'm absolutely puritanical and Lutheran about the stage directions, it doesn't make the people doing my plays any more rigorous in practice. . . . I began to have a mad desire to put in stage directions like 'something strange happens' or 'there's a furry pause.' Nobody ever got those wrong, but when I said, 'there's a door up left,' they always got that wrong."[1] If a playwright crafts texts the way that a shipwright crafts ships, then Wellman seems to be intentionally building in some holes below the waterline—just for the sheer pleasure of making a production bail frantically.

Reveling in Wellman's riddling, riddled comedy, though, mustn't detract from his gravity of purpose. He may never sound solemn, but he is serious.

These works constitute a realistic portrait of the world as he sees it: a perilous place that can't be negotiated without bravery, a mistrust of neatness, and a prehensile brain. How can any twentieth-century citizen not know how slippery words are? He writes during an administration that is managing to ward off the Geneva Convention semantically—simply by naming its foes "enemy combatants," a term found nowhere (and therefore protected nowhere) in international law. Cynicism and linguistic perversion do have consequences. Give something a new name: you can torture it.

In that 1984 manifesto, Wellman says, "In our time only bad artists name what they cherish, because what is cherished, or revered, or loved, will immediately be used as a tool by the powers that be."[2] He, therefore, works in double negatives and untied meanings. He conjures up monsters and names them with jabberwockian glee. (Adam never named half so many animals as the Devil did.) He poses as truth-telling imp, a prankster, the Loki of Brooklyn. And by painting himself as wicked, Wellman also avoids being what he loathes most—the playwright (or artist or New Yorker or citizen) as victim. The playwrights who have studied in his Pataphysics workshops or in his classes at Brooklyn College have begun to take this lightness and self-sufficiency for granted. Ann Marie Healy, Thomas Bradshaw, Anne Washburn, Madeleine George, Young Jean Lee, and a host of others now feel no compunction about violating Aristotelian rules that still (amazingly) hold sway in our stodgier theaters. Audiences go to him for similar training. Reading and watching by Wellman's Lucifer-light, we have to stay flexible and alert, never relaxing into "geezerly" emotions like self-pity. Wellman is only being bad to teach us to be good. Or, as his narrator muses in *Infrared,* "Being damned in this world amounts to / being blessed in the next is the / overriding theme of the event."

NOTES

1. Carrie Hughes, "A Play for a Broken World," *Theater* (Yale) 32, no. 2 (April 2002).

2. Mac Wellman, "The Theatre of Good Intentions," *Performing Arts Journal* 83 (1984).

Infrared

I went in search of myself.

—HERACLITUS

Infrared (a collaboration with artist and puppeteer Janie Geiser) was first presented at New York University in 1996 under the direction of Travis Preston. Subsequently, the play was presented by Fancy Pants at Dance Theater Workshop in 1999.

PERSONS OF THE PLAY

Our NARRATOR, an ungainly self in search of itself

CATHY X, a young woman with a shocking dual identity

CATHY X'S SHADOW, a spooky temporal disturbance with a mind of its own

WOW, her dog and trusted confidante

Various PASSERSBY, CRIMINALS, DISCIPLES OF CATHY X, and assorted HOLES and SHADOWS, including that of the Flatiron Building

THE SETTING

Infrared takes place in contemporary New York and in the Infrared mirror world, rendered spaciotemporally speaking, in a series of dioramas and puppet theaters of varying scale.

SCENE [HOLE ●]

An urban street corner just at the end of twilight. Shadows of tall buildings cut across our view. Street and sidewalk and the light of a looming half-moon. A strange, misshapen SILHOUETTE, *with shadow, appears, and we hear whatever it is speaking in a deep, husky half-whisper as voice-over.*

NARRATOR:

I suppose you would like to know who I am,
and if not "who" then "what."

Pause.

There is a problem with this.

Pause.

I don't *know* what I am, and I am not
sure there is a "who" to be found there,
or here, I mean.

Pause.

This worries me.

Pause.

This worries me because . . . well, let's just
say, it worries me, and leave it at that.

Pause.

When I was young I had no problems
with this attribute of my physiognomy.

Pause.

I was going to say, "When I was a kid," but
I'm not sure that's accurate.

Pause.

You see, I might have grown from a seed, a bulb,
or maybe even a piece of rotten fruit.

Pause.

My origin was amazement.

Pause.

I look up at the moon and witness
the light of my beginning. Folks are
afraid of me. Maybe they have good
reason to be.

Shadow of a claw scratching a horny head. We hear scratching noises.

My origin was in the bright, bright
cup of radiance that is starlight.
How else could I have come into being?
How else?

A LITTLE MAN *comes up with a cigarette.*

LITTLE MAN:
Hey, bud, got a light?

Sees the whole, vast bulk of our NARRATOR *and freezes in terror. As the latter's shadow swoops over the* MAN, *we hear a crunching noise. The shadow withdraws and the* LITTLE MAN *is squashed flat.*

NARRATOR:

I don't like interruptions, as you may have
noticed. Particularly when I am talking about
my origins. Alone of all things my origins
are dear to me.

We hear an ambulance and see people scurrying about.

All I recall of my youth, after the
bright moment of amazement, I mean,
was a clearing in the middle of a
forest. Birds were singing there,
deep in the heart of the woods. I was
smaller then, not so large and bulky.
A strange, sharp wiggle of a shadow.

Pause.

At times I felt as though I possessed
a tail. At times I felt as if I were
a tail. The tail wagging the dog
of some other existence.

Pause.

Nowadays it is difficult for me even
to turn around, so I cannot be sure
whether I possess a tail, or am one.

Pause.

If I am one, whatever I am the tail of
must be a prodigious monster, a
true swamp gahoon.

Pause.

I crept into the city via the Holland Tunnel.
Crept in from a region where paperclips
evolve into coat hangers, a world of nocturnal
cobwebbery.

Pause.

Obviously I had to be very careful.

Pause.

I did not want to attract too much attention,
so I chose the wee hours of the night
for my entrance and arrival.

Pause.

Even so, I was the occasion of much
amazement.

Pause.

The terror I cause is a hindrance in my
drive to understand myself. You others
who also seek self-understanding
surely can appreciate the knot of
my conundrum. What is self, after
all, but the series of approximate

responses to the darksome shadow
of self, the abyss of being? Being.
Are we not all mere reflections of . . .
of that primordial starburst of amazement?
Are we not all formed from our own
dense, unfathomable drives and the
myriad reactions occasioned in others
by these? Do we not all share the same
original stereopanopticon? Perhaps.
Perhaps not.

Pause.

My search for my self has been arduous,
difficult to describe. A hollow within a
cube within another hollow.

All the people, dogs, and cats have by now fled, leaving only their shadows. These merge with our NARRATOR*'s. Like a bag full of cats, it changes shape continually.*

That brings me to the point of my tale:
my shadow, apparently exasperated by my
difficult nature, unpleasant appearance,
and sheer superficial discontinuity
went stark raving mad. My shadow broke
off from me and merged with others,
the vulgar shadows of the hoi polloi—
those I had terrorized—the mob.

His shadow alters, becoming an oscillating imp of zany complexity, as if alive.

What could I do? Nothing but look on
from the filamentous crack of whatever
was left of me and the dark substance
of my dematerialized dark side—my id.
Waiting for the moment to make myself whole
once more. Waiting for the moment to strike.
And yet, I did not have to wait long.

The shadow breaks up into a series of nine smaller shadows, arranged in three rows of three. In turn, each of these darkens. The body of darkness drains out of each as they are transformed, one by one, into holes.

The fragments of my shadow had become a
crowd of kneeling holes, like an orderly
array of ardent disciples. Worshipping.
But, Lord knows, before what craven idol
did they worship?

Pause.

Perhaps it was the haze of moonlight.
Moonlight that recalls us to focus,
distance, and the love that permeates
all cavities so filled; perhaps it
was the detail of cracks and fissures
on the sidewalks and roadbeds, the
texture of these surfaces like the hand
of a familiar acquaintance; perhaps
it was the moon itself, for all the
world like an immaterial being—herself
adrift; perhaps it was the empty space
the moon and heavens are filled with,
nameless fillers, nameless bodies
of figures and grounds; I hardly knew.

Indeed, the holes are bowing slowly now before the silhouette of our now shadowless NARRATOR. *He groans.*

I may be wrong, but . . . but I think
they are worshipping me. My disciples.

Pause.

Amazing.

Pause.

Suddenly, however, it occurred to me
that I, too, am an empty—a vessel
of absence. The merest inscription
of nothingness, and as I realized
this, I could literally smell fear.

Pause.

I could smell fear and terror, twin
companions like my former shadow, and
my inability to escape the pseudosolid
into which I had been poured. This
oddly framed identity of mine: a
hollow within a cube within another
hollow.

The entire puppet theater suddenly fills with light then darkness.

This pseudosolid that I had grasped at,
like Orpheus at Eurydice.

Shadow of an arm and hand. Shadow of girl receding. A faraway scream.

Stranger yet, when I reached out to touch
my disciples crouched before me, crouched
before me neatly, in three rows of three,
my fingers could not feel . . . feel anything
there.

We see the shadows deepen as obvious holes.

I closed my eyes, and the tips of my fingers
sought out lovingly the shapes of those
who worshipped me, whom I also loved.
I reached for them but they were gone;
each shadow fallen into the mystery
of its own distinct but arbitrary—
unfathomable—hole.

A cloud passes over the moon. The motionless holes rest motionlessly.

I realized I would have to follow them
wherever they had gone. So, I selected
one (according to the ancient Rule
of Hollow and Shadow) while observing too
the contradictory laws of my own nature . . .

A flock of storks flies past the moon. A lone stork flies into the hole of the moon.

I went in search of myself . . . of whatever
it was I was looking for.

Pause.

For whatever it was I was looking for
was bigger game than a mere question
of nested holes.

A gloved hand reaches out and rolls a marble into one of the holes. Slow blackout as the music fades.

SCENE [DEPRESSION ⌣]

The same as before, only the moon is now three-quarters full. A rat runs across the street. A cat appears right behind, stalking. Both freeze. Headlights appear, and both scurry off. A sedan drives up, stops, parks. A man gets out, and a woman. They embrace, and the man waits until she gets in the door of her apartment. A light comes on in a window above, the woman appears and waves. The man waves back and returns to his car. Drives off—the shadow of the sedan remains, looks about, and thus notices other, similarly orphaned shadows. We hear our familiar NARRATOR *as voice-over.*

NARRATOR:

The shadow epigones of my own, nearly
perfect shadow had become a schizophrenic
multitude of kneeling holes. It appeared
to me they were involved in the act of . . .
of worship.

Pause.

If this be true, before what brazen image
did they fawn?

CHORUS OF SHADOWS:

We worship the solid that blocks out light, spooky;
We worship the tree branch, flickering schematically
against the hole of the moon, spooky;

We worship the wall, obdurate and unyielding
like the will of the Evil One, spooky;
We worship the sun-hat, sunglasses, and sunblock
of the sun-blinded, very cool yet unaccountable,
and spooky;
We worship the roof of the adjoining warehouse, dim
in the caverns of night, spooky;
We worship the passing automobile, with its evanescent
shadow, quite spooky;
We worship the rushing dog, with its long, frightening arabesque
of shadow, quite spooky;
We worship what shades us from our destroyer, X, the Light.

A SINGLE CHORISTER:

The Primal Shadow, and Father of our
amazement, loved to sit in the moonlight
and talk with the moon.

THE OLDEST SHADOW:

Hello, Moon, my old friend.

MOON:

Hello there. What are you doing down there?

THE OLDEST SHADOW:

I am keeping all things hinged to the doors and
windows of customary appearance. What are you
doing up there?

MOON:

Wouldn't you like to know, you . . . mediocre nonentity.

NARRATOR:

Perhaps, I thought to myself, it is the haze
of the moonlight that recalled me to focus,
distance, and the twisted love that permeates
all cavities so filled; perhaps it is the detail
of cracks and fissures on the sidewalks and roadbeds,
of a familiar acquaintance; perhaps, it is only
the moon, for all the world like an immaterial
being, herself adrift; perhaps it is the dark
matter the emptiness of the heavens is filled with . . .

CHORUS:

We, nameless filler, nameless bodies
of figure and ground; he hardly knew which.

NARRATOR:

I may be wrong, but . . . but I think they are
worshipping me, my sweet but lunatic disciples.

CHORUS:

Amazing.

A SINGLE CHORISTER:

Amazing, indeed.

We hear a strange and spooky laughter as the shadows begin turning into holes.

NARRATOR:

Suddenly, it occurred to me that I too
must be unredeemably empty, a vessel
of absence. The merest inscription
of nothingness and . . . and as I came

to this rude realization I could smell
fear.

A wolf howls, a bat crosses the moon. The moon drips blood. Pause.

I could smell fear and terror—the twin familiars
of my haunted, topological obsession—and my
inability to escape from this nightmarish
cabinet of illusion to which I had been exiled
seemed an unassailable fact. For now, even
without my shadow, I glimmered, glimmered
in the faint pseudosolid chiaroscuro of my
inner theater. And the shadowy knowledge
that I had grasped at . . .

The entire puppet theater suddenly fills with light, then darkness.

. . . had become Eurydice, the spectral girl
haunted Orpheus reached for in vain.

Shadow of an arm and hand. Shadow of girl receding. A faraway scream.

Stranger yet, when I reached out
to touch . . . I could not feel anything.

Pause.

I closed my eyes and the tips of my
fingers lovingly sought out the shapes
of those who worshipped me, whom I adored.

Light vampiric laughter. Clouds pass over the moon. The motionless holes sit, motionless.

I realized I would have to follow them
wherever they had gone, so I selected
the one that seemed most promising,
and observing the rule of nature . . .

A flock of pelicans flies past the moon. A lone pelican flies into the hole of the moon.

I went in search of whatever it was . . .
I was looking for.

A hand reaches out and rolls a marble into a hole. Total black. Pause.

I enter one of the holes and encounter
the world of Infrared.

Everything bursts into brightest scarlet, infrared. We hear strange infrared music. The scene is the same, only different. There are people milling about. One of them, a young woman, CATHY X, *and her dog. The* WOMAN *sits down at a park bench to read a book. Her shadow is a monster shadow. She looks at her hands oddly but makes nothing of it. Her dog,* WOW, *on the other hand, sensitive in doggy ways, notices something has changed. But what?*

CATHY X:

Wow, what's wrong? You look like you've seen
a ghost.

WOW:

Look at me, I'm different. All of a sudden
everything looks different, too. And your shadow!
Someone must have flipped the switch and slipped
over from the Other Side. Cathy, Cathy . . .

But she's reading her book. Now the Infrared shape of our NARRATOR *looms up just in front of the two.* WOW *is anxious about this.*

Oh, it's you. One of the . . . big ones . . . from the
Other Side. Uh-oh. Neither one of us is of any
importance. I'm an ordinary dog with ordinary
proclivities. Named Wow. She's an ordinary
dog owner of no importance. Named Cathy X.
Neither of us knows anything about anything
pertaining to the Other Side, and we possess
no abnormal proclivities. Ordinary girl. Dog.
Ordinary proclivities. Really.

NARRATOR:

An ordinary dog by the name of Wow?

She looks up surprised but not intimidated in the least.

CATHY X:

How did you know his name? That's his name,
but how did you know it? Are you psychic?
I have a friend down in Jersey City whose first
cousin has a Weimaraner named Wow. She's psychic.
Sandy Adler is her name, and she was married to
Pat Riley's brother-in-law—Pat Riley of the Knicks?
Only he's not manager of the Knicks no more.
You follow basketball? I don't follow basketball.
You can call me Cathy.

WOW:

Cathy X.

CATHY X:

Don't bark at the man, Wow. He may be psychic.

NARRATOR:

That shadow—

CATHY X:

Say hello to the man, Wow.

Suddenly noticing.

Wow, he's kindava . . . big guy . . .

WOW:

How do you do?

CATHY X:

Wow is an extraordinary dog.

NARRATOR:

That shadow—

CATHY X:

I, however, am a very ordinary person . . .
(Hey, why am I talking this way?) . . .
Ordinary girl, ordinary job, ordinary
proclivities, except for one extraordinary . . .
one single, solitary fact:

NARRATOR:

That shadow—

CATHY X:

My shadow.

Pause.

My shadow got too big.

NARRATOR:

That shadow is my shadow.

CATHY X'S SHADOW:

I am her shadow, the shadow of Cathy X, and
I know many things about her, and Wow also,
since I frequently am one with his shadow also.

Pause.

NARRATOR:

That shadow is my shadow.

CATHY X:

Mister, I don't think your elevator goes
all the way to the top. Go away or I'll
call the police.

NARRATOR:

Madame, I have no interest in you. But
there is a matter I wish to take up with
your semblable.

CATHY X:

Semblable?

NARRATOR:

The image of your obscure space, as seen
cutting across a surface, and rendered thus
almost an object. It belongs, in part, to me.

CATHY X'S SHADOW:

Okay. Okay. I'll meet you later. At Zigzag.
We'll straighten it out. Okay. Now, beat it.

CATHY X:

My shadow, you mean.

Pause.

Look, I don't mean to be unsympathetic
but I don't understand what you mean.
I'm sorry, but there's nothing I can do.

Pause. Our NARRATOR *turns away in despair.*

NARRATOR:

In my despair, I turned away
from Cathy X. I turned away
from her shadow. I turned away
even, from her dog, Wow.
I made a prayer to my aloneness:

Pause.

O Holy One, X, My Destroyer and Savior,
Please take away the shoes
Of those who opened my eyes
To the radiance of Infrared.
Remind them of my presence
So I may grow another shadow
As dark as the one they
Stole from me in my innocence.
Place them in the hole of Time
Along with Time's junk.

Pause.

Place them there so they will leave
Me alone.

SCENE [GROOVE V]

Full, red moon. Same as before: CATHY X, *her* SHADOW, WOW, *and our* NARRATOR; *also, life-size in adjoining dioramas,* CATHY X *herself, and behind the scrim, the dim and menacing figure of our* NARRATOR. *Action happens simultaneously in both the micro (puppet theater) and macro (diorama) worlds.*

NARRATOR:

You thought I'd never find you.
You thought no one from my world
could ever find you here, here
in the world of Infrared.

CATHY X'S SHADOW: *(aside)*

Let's just say I was counting on it.

CATHY X:

I don't know what you're talking about.

NARRATOR:

You know who I am, and why I'm here.
Don't play stupid.

CATHY X:

All I know is you're as big as a house,
and you don't look right. You don't
even look human.

CATHY X'S SHADOW:

That's the way. The classic counterpunch.
Ask him, "Is he human?" Do it.

CATHY X:

Are you human? What are you?
You're not, are you?

NARRATOR:

Maybe. Maybe I'm not.

CATHY X'S SHADOW:

"Maybe!" Ha!

NARRATOR:

Maybe in your terms I am an . . . aberration
of nature.

CATHY X'S SHADOW:

That's a dandy circumlocution. Don't
you mean "a monster"?

NARRATOR:

Yes, a monster.

CATHY X:

Well, why don't you go back where you came
from and just leave me alone?

NARRATOR:

I won't go till I get my shadow back.

CATHY X:

Look, there must be some mistake.

NARRATOR:

There is no mistake. You have stolen
my shadow. I am from the Other Side,
and you or your disciples have, with
or without your knowledge, committed
an act of felonious assault upon the
person of my shadow.

CATHY X'S SHADOW:

Well, lah-dee-dah! It's quite the learned
monster. Fucking dinosaur. Fucking reptile.

NARRATOR:

Tell me your real name.

CATHY X'S SHADOW:

Don't tell him a damn thing.

CATHY X:

My name is a matter of no importance.
I'm an ordinary young person with certain
ordinary proclivities, and an ordinary dog.

CATHY X'S SHADOW:

That's good. Calm. Defiance in the face
of intimidation.

CATHY X:

Say hello to the man . . . to the . . .
whatever it is. Wow. Say hello.

WOW:

How do you do, Monsoor?

NARRATOR:

Hello, Wow.

WOW:

I am quite the fierce little fellow,
though sensitive beyond the merely
canine. Her name is Cathy X . . .

CATHY X'S SHADOW:

Don't . . . don't you fool . . .

WOW:

She works as a semipermanent temp
at Acme Products Incorporated, a
small wholesale distributor, there,
in the Flatiron Building. She lives
with me in an illegal sublet in the
East Village. It's a hole, but it's
home. The landlord wants us out.

An anxious New York moment.

Except for him, we're not a threat
to anyone. She's clean, polite, and tidy,
not to mention politically naive.

NARRATOR:

I do not understand—what is this
thing called "politically naive"?

WOW:

Downtown theater. Depressing, but harmless.

Pause.

Now, what she doesn't know is that
Acme Products is the front for some
pretty sinister arms' racketeers.
With contacts in Teheran, Tel Aviv,
and Foggy Bottom, of course. The
real point of the enterprise is
the purchase, final machining, and—
ultimately, of course—exportation
(highly illegal!) of various oddly
shaped and perforated donuts, cups,
and stranger rebuses of more or less
pure zirconium and beryllium.

CATHY X'S SHADOW: *(aside)*
I can't believe it! Is honor dead?!

NARRATOR:
Zirconium? What's that?

WOW:
And beryllium, too. For cladding.
It is to be made into cladding, and
otherwise employed in the manufacture
of miniaturized nuclear devices.
Bombs.

A gasp from everyone, except CATHY X.

A gulf of unspeakable danger
looms beneath the lightest of her
footsteps. A crater of doom.

CATHY X'S SHADOW:

Doom for you all, barred from grace
by a hole.

WOW:

Barred from grace by the shadow
of fear.

CATHY X'S SHADOW:

Blasphemer.

WOW growls.

NARRATOR:

I don't believe it.

CATHY X'S SHADOW:

I don't believe you either.

SHADOW OF THE FLATIRON BUILDING:

Wow is telling the truth. I am the shadow
of the Flatiron Building, anonymous and
even more terrifying than the Ugly One,
there. My footprint covers nearly a whole
city block—and my host, the Flatiron
Building, is full of copying machines,
cold pizza in wax paper wedged into the
bottoms of wastepaper baskets, stubs
of pencils, paperclips, and nameless horror.
It is full to the top with copying machines
and other junk. Junk like the junk in
time's hole. You are all politically naive.

NARRATOR:

I don't believe you either.

SHADOW OF THE FLATIRON BUILDING:

You have dug a trench of ignorance
around yourselves and climbed down into it.

WOW backs off in terror and is devoured by CATHY X's SHADOW. This event is witnessed by a passerby, an OLD MAN, who yells in alarm. An OLD WOMAN is attracted by the commotion and rushes up.

CATHY X:

Wow, where are you?

OLD MAN:

Lady, your dog—it, well, it disappeared.

NARRATOR:

No, it didn't, you moron, it got eaten by her
shadow. Just like it ate mine.

CATHY X'S SHADOW:

Guess I showed that little fucker.

The OLD MAN is terrified. He faints.

CATHY X:

You scared him. See what you did?

CATHY X'S SHADOW:

See what you did, you big ape. Ha!

OLD WOMAN:

That was no shadow, buster. That's a
hole disguised as a shadow.

CATHY X:

Sometimes I hate New York City. Here
I am, a perfectly normal young woman.
With a perfectly normal life, perfectly
normal needs and proclivities. About
$212 in the bank, a more or less
loathsome job doing temp work at . . .
never mind . . .

Exasperated.

And my dog disappears. Eaten by a shadow.

OLD WOMAN:

A shadow ate my husband, Morton, but
nobody believed me, honey, it's true.

SHADOW OF THE FLATIRON BUILDING:

Whose shadow was it?

MOON:

That was no shadow, Cathy.

OLD MAN: *(coming to)*

I am a normal-type tax-paying citizen.
I don't want to get involved.

NARRATOR:

Be quiet, fool.

OLD MAN: *(to CATHY X)*

I didn't see nothing, lady, I swear.

OLD WOMAN:

Shaddup. Can't you see by the way she's
talking? Her elevator don't go all the
way to the top.

SHADOW OF THE FLATIRON BUILDING:

Just what is that supposed to mean?

MOON:

Yeah, just what are you insinuating?

OLD WOMAN:

Aw crap.

CATHY X:

But . . . but . . .

MOON:

Cathy, listen to your inner ratiocinator.

She perks up.

Cathy, which of all these shadows seems the
most . . . unusual?

CATHY X:

Right now, I'd say all of them.

MOON:

Look carefully.

She eyes her own SHADOW *suspiciously. It tries to make itself small.*

CATHY X'S SHADOW:

What are you staring at? I didn't
do anything. Cut it out.

MOON:

Yes, it is your own shadow that is
the most . . . peculiar, is it not?

NARRATOR:

That's because her shadow has stolen
my shadow and turned it into a hole.

MOON:

Quiet, let her reply.

But CATHY *is speechless.*

OLD MAN:

Nutcase.

OLD WOMAN:

Psycho.

They trundle off.

MOON:

Yes, Cathy, it is your own shadow
that is the most unusual, is it not?

CATHY X:

Well, yes. Kinda big and lumpy.

CATHY X'S SHADOW:

I resent the insinuation.

MOON:

What else?

CATHY X:

Strange. Definitely strange.

CATHY X'S SHADOW:

. . . mnmph . . .

MOON:

Do you not perceive how your own shadow seems unnatural? As though it were not you who threw it, slithering maniacally along the coarse surface of the sidewalk . . .

NARRATOR:

That's because it's mine.

MOON:

Be quiet, Big Fella!—slithering maniacally along the sidewalk and pavement, but were some other, truly demonic being of a color our eyes are not accustomed to. Do you not notice these things?

CATHY X:

Now that you mention it.

Touches the SHADOW with her foot.

Hey, there's nothing there.

Sure enough: it's a hole.

VOICES FROM HER SHADOW:

(a) Cathy, Cathy—listen . . .

(b) Listen to us, we're your friends . . .

(c) Follow your hunch. You've got
nothing to lose . . .

(a) . . . but your doggy . . .

All laugh lightly. Pause. Gingerly she touches and tastes. Nothing.

CATHY X:

Hell, there's nothing in here, only
empty space. A hole. Hey, it's
just an empty cavity. Wow.

WOW: *(from within the hole)*

Cathy, it's me . . . I'm lost in here.

She moves toward her insane SHADOW. *The* SHADOW *quivers with excitement.*

CATHY X'S SHADOW:

Come to me, my sweet. Let us make
music together. The mystic cadenza
of the night.

CATHY X:

Wow, if you don't mind, I think I'll
just wait out here. Till you come back.

A DARK FIGURE *emerges and reaches for her. She is frozen with fear.*

NARRATOR:

Be ye shadow or be ye hole, you
owe me my due. I want my shadow
back. Now.

The SHADOW *turns darkly to our* NARRATOR. *Pause. They stare at one another.*

CATHY X'S SHADOW:

Stay out of this, you fool.

Insensibly, CATHY X *is lured into her own* SHADOW, *and we hear a celestial music.*

I am her True Intentionality, her higher purpose,
which even she, in her girlish political
naïveté, cannot fathom.

NARRATOR:

I will not be denied.

CATHY X'S SHADOW:

You have lost your shadow because of a
defect of the soul.

NARRATOR:

A defect of the soul?

CATHY X'S SHADOW:

A thing lacking in your spaciotemporal
identity. You have been a phantom to
the world, now you are a phantom to
yourself.

Pause. A monsterly sob.

NARRATOR:

Am I to be utterly forsaken?

CATHY X'S SHADOW:

No, for even you shall be redeemed by
Our Saviour.

NARRATOR:

Our Saviour?! Ha ha ha. I lost my faith
way back, along with my cornball innocence.
All that's a fraud. An atavistic puppet
show. It may play in Peoria, but I don't
buy it.

CATHY X'S SHADOW:

That monstrous arrogance is the defect
I was speaking of, you fool.

NARRATOR:

I was born in amazement—the complex
rules of the Big City are my opiate.

CATHY X'S SHADOW:

Bars across the window of your hopes and
dreams. Your complexity is a prison.

NARRATOR:

I don't believe you.

CATHY X'S SHADOW:

Never mind! Cathy is suffering a shadow-
change into something rich and strange.

Presently, when she reemerges in her
full glory, you will see there is room
in her Holy diadem even for a puffed-up
deluded apostate such as you.

NARRATOR:

What I want is simple.

CATHY X'S SHADOW:

Her name is Catherine X no more; She
is now a Catherine wheel of our Salvation;
X, the crisscross of the Mini-Maximal;
X, the site of our human transcendence,
and our passing over into Wild Time;
X, where shadow and hole are annihilated
in the love which possesseth no moniker.

NARRATOR:

This is uncanny—now I'm even more
scared than before.

The DARK FIGURE *pauses, then reenters the hole of* CATHY X'S SHADOW.

Damnation. Now I'm lost. Forever.

A giant fist smashes on the pavement. A cat leaps from roof to roof. A dog below barks. A horde of evil insects skitters across the street as a cloud passes over the face of the moon. She, CATHY X, *emerges as a goddess with* WOW *in attendance.*

CATHY X:

Yes, my poor eremite. You were correct
in your guess. I am X, the Destroyer.
And yes, my shadow has taken your shadow.

NARRATOR:

Well, I want it back.

CATHY X:

All in good time. All in good time. First
I shall enlighten you concerning the true
nature of shadows and holes. Please be seated.

Pause.

My, what large and horny feet you possess.

The ground shakes as our NARRATOR *sits down.*

NARRATOR:

And I listened to her speak.
And her beauty made me dumb.
And what she spoke was the gospel
of the Evil One.

Candles appear in all the holes. Mist. Bats. Cats, dogs, and people all assemble at her feet. Pause. She moves the little toe of her left foot. All move the little toes of their respective left feet.

CHORUS:

And she is covered with cobweb, shoelace, and golden thread;
And she is covered with tuft of mouse hair, thistle, and niter.

Repeat and etc.

NARRATOR:

And I knew she had possessed my shadow
    for some profound reason;

And I knew it was hers to take, and that she
must have it;
And I was grateful that she had found my shadow
comely, since I was big, brutish, and despised
among my own kind;
And her soft hair glittered in the moonlight
like the scales of the dragon;
And I knew that although I was the most abject and
wretched of creatures, I should in the fullness
of time grow a new shadow, and that this shadow
would be wondrous and its name would be "wormwood"
and its name would be "maniacal slitherer" and . . .

Slow blackout.

SCENE [CAVITY ✻]

Full moon as before. X, *the Destroyer, and her dog,* WOW, *surrounded by disciples and curious bystanders, quietly preaches the gospel to the inhabitants of the world of Infrared—at the corner of 23rd Street and Broadway. We see our* NARRATOR*'s silhouette and hear his prayer from the end of the previous scene.*

NARRATOR:

And she is covered with cobwebbery, shoelaces, and the
ears of mice;
And she is tufted with thistles, feathers, and niter, and
the soft fur of moles;
And I know she has possessed my shadow
for some profound reason;
And I know it is hers to take, and that she must
have it;
And I am grateful that she has found my shadow
comely, since I am big, brutish, and thoroughly

despised among my own kind;
And her soft hair glitters in the moonlight
like the sparkling scales of the dragon;
And I knew that although I was the most wretched
and abject of creatures, I shall in the fullness
of time grow a new shadow, and this shadow shall
be wondrous and its name shall be "wormwood"
and its name shall be "maniacal slitherer"
and its name shall be "the Great Dork" and
its name shall be "Prince Zandor" and its name
shall be "Monsoor Shade" and its name shall
be "Catherine Wheel" and . . . and . . .

Now we hear her sermon.

CATHY X:

PEOPLE and animals do certain things
because they believe they have come
across a hole, because they want to
dig a hole, to pass through a hole, to
jump over a hole, or to hide inside one.

Pause.

HOLES, like shadows and persons, are
spaciotemporally localized beings. And
like these too, they may best be thought
of as temporary disturbances.

Pause.

HOLES, like shadows, have hosts and, like
shadows, are dependent upon these for existence.

Pause.

HOLES and shadows, like the lilies of the field,
toil not; they accompany us in our labors and in
our pleasures; they remind us of the insubstantiality
of our vainglorious wishful thinking.

Pause.

AND so I came out of a world on the Other Side
in order to redeem you all, the lost ones,
from the folly of your ways; for it is the
folly and wretchedness of the inhabitants
of Infrared that you are always mistaking
wrong for right; just as you mistake holes
for shadows and shadows for holes.

Pause.

AND it is my task to set the matter right
and show you the way to redemption is paved
with the stones of mercy and forgiveness,
stones that sparkle like the scales of the dragon . . .

NARRATOR:
Pardon me.

CATHY X:
Yes, my child.

NARRATOR:
Owing to a defect of the soul, I have suffered
the loss of my shadow; also, I have become large
and scary, and covered with horns. And horny-type
protuberances . . .

CATHY X:

So I see.

NARRATOR:

Are there miracles you know of
that may enable a return to my
proper state?

She looks at him and smiles. An odd shadow appears. It zigzags sharply.

CATHY X:

Consider the inchworm. What a little devil
of a shadow it possesses, yet it is meek
and does no harm.

NARRATOR:

Some devil of a hole has swallowed my shadow,
and I have come from the Other Side, here,
to the land of Infrared, to get it back.

CATHY X:

Be not wrathful. Be not wroth.

NARRATOR:

I am not wroth, I am angry.

CATHY X:

The two are the same.

Pause.

CONSIDER what it is the inchworm measures
with his ridiculous lurch-and-drag walk;
he measures his way down the aeons of unproof;
he measures nothing that is not a thought

of God; he measures his life that it may be shared with all; he shares his joy with sensitive touches; he shares his finitude with all the great works of infinity; he measures the love of Time for the small motions of the soul, ever-seeking, ever-grasping, ever-blind. The inchworm's love measures out an infinity of bliss, inch by inch, unconcerned, unself-conscious, unable to refrain from enacting the work of making Holy. Study the inchworm.

NARRATOR: *(aside)*

But as she spoke, a wicked thought came into my mind. But as I could not form a sentence to express that thought, I said only,

(to CATHY X)

But I am wretchedness incarnate . . .

CATHY X:

Even you, in your wretchedness, shall possess the gift of sparkle.

NARRATOR:

But I am uncouth and clumsy.

CATHY X:

Study refinement and the relation between the insane zigzag of the inchworm's shadow and the tidiness of the inchworm's hole.

WOW has been sniffing at the inchworm and now begins barking at it.

Wow, stop it. Wow.

NARRATOR:

But I have lost my shadow—or someone has
stolen it; I have stepped into a hole of deep
despair; I have followed a tunnel of despair
until I have found my way here.

CATHY X:

If you would but surrender your shadow
to its fate, it would not be changed into
a hole.

NARRATOR:

Holes frighten me.

CATHY X:

Holes are friends. They mark the way out.

NARRATOR:

They way out of what?

CATHY X:

Out of our common woe.

NARRATOR:

Maybe I've been mistaken. Tell me more.

CATHY X:

My message is a simple one: give away
everything you own, and take to the open road
preaching the gospel of mercy and forgiveness.

NARRATOR: *(aside)*

But as X spoke, a strange thing happened
in my heart of hearts: I realized suddenly

that if she were X, I must be Y, a Judas-man
and the type of the True Destroyer; I realized
that I was an imp—the true quintessential imp
of Double Negative: I realized, in my desperate
aloneness, that it was to be my lot to kiss
her. To kiss X upon the cheek and so betray her.

He kisses her. A brief commotion. It stops. All people, animals, shadows, and holes stare at him, astonished.

CATHY X:

So, it is you.

NARRATOR:

I did not know it until now.

CATHY X:

So, you are the one.

NARRATOR:

I have betrayed you.

CATHY X:

Tell me, Monsoor Y, for that must be your
name, why have you done this act? What have
I done that you would betray me?

NARRATOR:

I do not know why. And that is the whole
of it. And the shadow of the whole of it
shall cut crookedly across the ruined fortress
of my face for all time.

CATHY X:

You do not know why, and that is the whole of it.

She kisses him back. WOW *barks.*

I forgive you, Monsoor Y, though you have murdered me.

All fade as we drift out of the world of Infrared.

SCENE [TUNNEL λ]

Same as before. Just before dawn. The red moon is far on the wane; it sits on its side, as though the wind had blown it over.

NARRATOR:

But as X spoke, a strange thing happened in my heart of hearts: I realized suddenly that if she were X, I was Y, a Judas-man and the true type of the Destroyer. I realized that I was an insidious, perverted imp—the quintessential Imp of ultimate Double Negative. I realized in my desperate aloneness that it was my lot to kiss X upon the cheek and so betray her.

CATHY X:

So, it is you.

NARRATOR:

I did not know it was me until now.

CATHY X:

So, you are the one.

NARRATOR:

I have betrayed you.

CATHY X:

Tell me, tell me, Monsoor Y—for that must
be your name—why have you done this act? What
harm have I done to you that you would betray
me?

NARRATOR:

I do not know why. And that is the whole
of it. And the shadow of the whole of it
shall cut crookedly across the ruined fortress
of my face till all time and love have come to dust.

CATHY X:

You do not know why, and that is
the whole of it.

She kisses him back. WOW *wags his tail.*

I forgive you, Monsoor Y, though
you have murdered me.

She turns away, then turns back.

As for my shadow, if you want it
so badly, you may have it. And surely
you will have need of one where you are
going.

CATHY X'S SHADOW:

No, no. Please, no. What have I done
to deserve this? Anything but this.
I'd rather be effaced for all time
by your radiance, than hang off of this . . .
no-account jerk . . . fucking swamp gahoon . . .
this miserable . . . Judas-man. No, no . . .

All fades as we drift out of the world of Infrared back into ours.

NARRATOR:

As we kissed, everything faded from sight,
and I drifted out . . . out of the world
of Infrared.

We're back home. A hawk flies across the moon. A cat chases a dog across the street.

Back home . . . the big city I knew and loved.
With its familiar sounds and smells.

A thick cloud of greasy smoke rolls down the street. A very tall MAN *is shooting baskets in an alleyway.* A LITTLE MAN *with* A BIG DOG *begins cursing* A BIG MAN *with* A LITTLE DOG.

LITTLE MAN:

Fuck you, Joey, you miserable fuck. I'll fucking
kill you, you stupid fuck. You owe me, Joey, and
you'd better come up with the dough. See, I'm
tight with some real mean guys over in Jersey,
and these guys would love an excuse to rearrange
your face, Joey.

Both DOGS *begin to piss.*

You understand what I'm saying, Joey? You had better
did. That's all I can say. And that hound of yours,
why that is the most miserable excuse of a mutt I've
ever seen. Is that some kind of grotesque growth
on his face? Just looking at that mutt is enough to
make me want to puke.

The BIG MAN *knocks over the* LITTLE MAN *and begins to kick him until the latter lies still. As the* LITTLE DOG *chews on the fallen* MAN*'s pant leg, the* BIG DOG *attacks the* BIG MAN *and drives him away. All through this the other* MAN *continues shooting baskets.* PEOPLE *appear in windows and shout.*

ANGRY INSOMNIACS:

(a) Hey, keep it down!
(b) Shut up, you hooligan! Vicious swine!
(c) Do you mind? I'm trying to get some sleep!

A HOMELESS PERSON *pushes a shopping cart slowly. Sees the dead man's shoes and carefully removes them. As he does, music begins, heralding the first light of dawn in the east. A manhole in the street pops up and bright light flashes up. One by one, the disciples of X, the Destroyer and Savior, appear and set up a long table for the Holy Banquet. Our* NARRATOR *talks over this.*

NARRATOR:

I never did figure out who or what I am.
Guess I don't mind too much. You don't
really need to know, at least not for
most purposes at life's little puppet show . . .

He laughs dryly.

And besides, I might turn out to be something
. . . something not all that appetizing . . .

and wouldn't that be an embarrassment?
Anyway, I've got my shadow back, even
if—let's just say—it's borrowed,
and it's just as wild and creepy as ever.
They're setting places at the table for
the Holy Banquet. X is both Destroyer
and Savior, it turns out. I don't know
what's on the plate, but I guess I'll
eat whatever it is along with the rest.
No complaints from me. Nosirree.
Being damned in this world amounts to
being blessed in the next is the
overriding theme of the event. I'm
not too clear on all of this, but I
figure I've got some catching up to
do, in the eschatology department.

Pause. Our Savior, CATHY X, *appears.* HER DISCIPLES *take charge and begin dressing her for her new role. All this is quite a shock since, unlike the* CATHY X *of* Infrared, *she seems unaware of her divine nature. As she is transformed, she talks a little with our* NARRATOR.

CATHY X:

You think you're perplexed.

NARRATOR:

Sometimes I'd like the world to go away.
Both of 'em.

Pause.

Maybe I've dug a trench of ignorance
around myself, and climbed down into it.

CATHY X:

I feel like that a lot, too. Stick of gum?

NARRATOR:

Sure. Thanks.

He takes it. Both chew meditatively.

CATHY X:

I'm not sure how long this current sublet
is going to last. I'd go back home to Mahwah,
but my sister's suicidal, and my brother
Richie is a creep.

NARRATOR:

I think I know your brother Richie.

CATHY X:

Everybody knows my brother Richie
since he knocked up that slut from
Staten Island, Gloria Fishman.

Pause.

NARRATOR:

Life in the city is . . . hard.

CATHY X:

Life in the city . . . oh well . . .

Completes her transformation as DISCIPLES *place a tiara of candles upon her head. Her miniature at the banquet table stands and delivers the sermon.*

PEOPLE and animals do certain things
because they believe they have come
across a hole, because they want to
dig a hole, to pass through a hole,
to jump over a hole, to get out of a
hole, or hide inside one . . .

She goes on as before, but we hear our NARRATOR.

NARRATOR:

All this seems so strangely familiar to me.
All this I know, as if by déjà vu, from some
other world linked to this one by Time's
worm-hole, and there is so much I want to
learn. So much to learn. Before . . . before
they come for me, as I am certain they will.
Because of the shadow, the shadow that was
not mine, that I brought with me all the
way from the world of Infrared . . .

In truth, the SHADOW *is acting like a bag full of schizophrenic alley cats. An ominous black sedan pulls up. The sedan is filled with dark red light. Two* MEN *dressed in black get out. They both carry blackjacks and are masked. Our* NARRATOR *doesn't see them, but his* SHADOW *does and quakes with fear.*

I want to learn why a thing can resemble
another thing, but not be at all the same;
I want to know where our dreams come from,
and how it is possible for us to desire things
that injure us, or drive us mad; I want to
know what the true limits of the human condition
are—and how we are to know when we have gone
too far—when we have disappeared into the

hole of our own undoing; I want to know why
I have become so disfigured that I cannot bear
my own image, and even my own shadow is a
visual horror to me; I want to know what love
is, and why when you reach to hold it, it flies
off in terror like the uncaged parakeet,
confused by sudden freedom: I want so badly
to know why oh why is there anything at all . . .

The masked MEN *quickly grab him from under his cloak, throw him in a big coal sack, and toss the sack into the trunk of the car. They get in and hurriedly drive off.*

NARRATOR'S SHADOW:

I suppose you would like to know who I am,
and if not "who," then "what."

Pause.

There is a problem with this.

As he goes on with the speech from the beginning of the play, lights slowly come down, except on the head of X, as we return to her sermon on the streets.

CATHY X:

FOR all things are Holy to me—see that
you follow the way of your Y to the
site of your X, for that hollow will be
the place of your hallowing;
FOR I am called X, and dwell in the holes
of fire you call Sun and Moon; and in all
the blazing, starry holes that the night
is drilled with;

FOR I both create and destroy according to
an ancient Rule of Hollow and Shadow;
FOR my joy is complex, and the Double Negative
of my fury raises the delectable flame
of desire in all the hearts of the Holy;
FOR I am both near and far—feel my breath
and fingertips on your cheek and on the
nape of your neck;
FOR I am difficult to grasp;
FOR any natural act, if hallowed, leads to me;
and nature needs people for what no angel
can perform—its hallowing—and in especial,
the hallowing of its hollows and holes.

Blackout.

End of play.

Jennie Richee; or, Eating Jalooka Fruit before It's Ripe

All our reasoning comes down to surrendering to feeling.

—PASCAL

Jennie Richee (based on the life and work of Henry Darger) was first presented in 2000 by the Ridge Theater in New York at St. Ann's under the direction of Bob McGrath and Laurie Olinder, through generous grants from the Rockefeller and Greenwall Foundations.

PERSONS OF THE PLAY

HENRY DARGER, in several incarnations, that is, on his deathbed, as various GENERALS and HEROES, as the bumbling PRIVATE, and as the aspiring artist, PENROD

The seven VIVIAN GIRLS, notably VIOLET, who sings all the songs

Various GLANDELINIAN and ABBEINIAN officers, flunkeys, and factotums

And lastly, various BLENGIGLOMENEAN creatures (or BLENGINS), both in their serpent and little girl forms

APROPOS OF *JENNIE RICHEE*

This theater piece is largely based on the personal, highly idiosyncratic work of outsider artist Henry Darger (1892–1973). The author has made extensive use of the many texts Darger employed in his picture making, but also on his own epic *Life History* (1966–73) and his extensive chronicles of the weather.

The text, thus, consists of a largely collaged attempt to trace some outlines of the development of Darger's remarkable artistic and spiritual achievement. Scenic notes and dialogic elements are often merged, partly to suggest something about the intrinsic seamlessness of Darger's vision (at least as apprehended by this author), and partly to challenge and inspire a certain specificity of scenic, visual, choreographic, and musical choices for the production. This procedure follows in the path of the author's *Hypatia,* which was staged with remarkable effect by Ridge Theater in their spring 1999 production with ART Institute students.

Thus, this text may have something of the appearance of a poem for the theater, which in a sense is what it is. This should in no way suggest that the author intends anything vague, atmospheric, or pretentiously "poetic"; indeed, the presentation laid out in the text is meant to imply a rigorous, minutely imagined theatrical texture, a texture as meticulously rendered as the magnificent pictures that are, in a sense, its subject.

Part 1: What Am I Doing in This Picture? begins with a mix of biographical elements, often from text or fragments of Darger's writings, particularly the *Life History;* Part 2: Carpets continues the narrative into that of Darger's immense novel, *The Realms Of The Unreal,* and we begin to encounter larger sections and whole scenes from his pictorial oeuvre; Part 3: Caverns continues this exploration and leads to a concluding celebration of Darger's achievement and the poignancy of his own end.

NOTE

Jennie Richee has been conceived by all those involved as a dense and complex multimedia theatrical event; the text presented here is only one part of the anticipated, final mix of elements. As with any project of this complexity, one or more elements may undergo considerable metamorphosis during the evolution of the piece.

The occasional appearance of an asterisk in the middle of a speech indicates that the next speech begins to overlap at that point. The overlapping speeches are all clearly marked in the text.

PART 1: WHAT AM I DOING IN THIS PICTURE?

Whiteness. A cube of
whiteness. A cylinder rolls to
reveal the old man a
young man enters. We found your
pictures, Henry. We found your
pictures.

~

He smiles. It's too late.

~

Music. We notice a dark dark cloud an
oval off to the right of the

a girl with
giant strawberry a girl with
an umbrella a girl with ram's horns
all three rush on. Stop

Girl with ram's horns. That is
going to be a cloudburst. Girl
with an umbrella. I hope the
wind won't pull my umbrella out of
my hands.

A sign appears beneath the third.
This is not a strawberry she is carrying.

Silence. Pause. Silence.

Someone does something.

We found your pictures, Henry.
Old man smiles a crinkled smile.

It's too late, he says.

General Henry Jose Dargerius, a hero, appears.
He is speaking in the Brazilian language
because back in 1905, of a doctor's diagnosis:
Little Henry's heart is not in the right place
River Aronburg Run has its
source from Lake Zannagustapolier.
River Angelina Run has its source
from Lake Prostentiateneha.

Primmaradia. Primanadia or
Mangaloo Crater.

~

The Hero speaks. Seven little girls listen.
They are hidden in this picture. Once,
not knowing any better I put
lots of newspaper beside the stove
near the wall, and set it on fire.

. . .

When this battle broke out called the battle
of Silver Bell the blue abyss of the sky
seemed to have yawned over the world
more deeply than ever before. The
Glandelinians at Fortress Silver Bell
had thought from the usual quietude
that nothing unusual was going to happen
but a sudden change touched the beautiful
scene.

. . .

The swaying shadow of some vast motion . . .

There had been queer sounds far away
early in the day and then there had seemed
far to the right in front a whole mountain
of smoke and debris
seemed to rise bodily up at the sky,
the wrinkled horizon line of landscapes not far
from the christian positions
seemed lifted to a straight line, the line
far away darkened and approached . . .

a monstrous, immeasurable
fold of purple motion
moving

as swift as a cloud shadow pursued by
sunlight.

~

We
see
sky,
with
lots
of weather
in it.

April 30 Saturday 1960. Rain
from 6 to 11 A.M. Cloudy
rest of the day.
7 to 9 P.M. 63 degrees. 11 A.M.
64 degrees. 5 to 6 P.M.
40 degrees. Some darn
drop indeed and this season

is called Spring? Spring.
Heavy de horse radish.

Went to mass; no tantrums.

The Hero speaks. Plenty of tantrums all day.
Three morning masses. One afternoon one.
Life history.
The Vivian girls speak for him. I got it
good once again from my father
when he thought from my actions that
I was going to do it again.
But I had no intention of doing so.

Everything stops.

Silence. A flower drifts by

Every 4th of July I shot off all
types of firecracker and never was
hurt or injured once, I was ever so
careful.
I was also crazy about making
bonfires but was so careful. I was
never scorched, singed, or burned. I
also loved to splash water at pools
left by rain especially with my hand
to pretend it was raining but somehow
I never got wet.

~

Blengins at corners of the sky
(Blengins are the ones with wings).

One thing I must say is that us
children in those days were
looked on as beneath the dignity

the worst to think of

of grownups and did not amount
to much where as to my opinion
or feeling all grownups, and especially
all types of strangers, and those I
did not like were less than the dust
or mud beneath my feet.

Blengins make the picture:
Sacred heart; Explosion.
I also had believed that I had read
in the Holy Bible, that children especially
all good and innocent ones
were more important to god
than the grownups, and that he,
when on earth as man, Jesus Christ,
had said that it was better for a man
or any person of any kind, if
harming a child, to have millstones

(not feathers)

to be tied around his neck
and be drowned in the depths of the
sea.

Someone holds a sign. And not feathers.

Or
the child guardian angel
will witness against the person
who harms a child
before god who is in heaven

Also in my boyhood days

(I was a little devil, if called "kid")

I had a very queer way of playing
in the snow,

by motion. All do this. By motion
of my left hand,

which later on got me into some
some serious trouble, of which
I will explain somewhat later.

~

Do you believe it, unlike most children,
I hated to see the day come when I will be
a grownup.
I never wanted to.
I wished to be young always.
I am grown up now and an
old lame man, darn it.

WILL THE WORLD EVER KNOW the
real dimensions of this disaster of the
war?

which crushed the fighting
christian forces at Delight's Junction
and left them broken and most disconsolate
and discouraged like a wounded dove or
seagull fluttering on the sandy beach
of the ocean

. . .

and the small but beautiful beachy shore
of the Sunbeam Creek
or river near Delight's Junction?

That once most beautiful river beach,
with its long stretches of strangely yet
unusually white sand, where long before
the war country children used to come
and play

. . .

What in the world had become of it.

Horribly misshapen, unusually
and strangely distorted, blotched
beyond comprehension
and drabbled
and horribly crimsoned,
and wreckage and body strewn

it
spread away to the north and south,
its ugly scars and shell holes and craters
made by explosions rendered more hideous
by the glinting rays of the winter sun.

~

Something is unscrolled. Something partly
revealed. We hear shapes and voices.
What
is going on down there, Violet?
Let's maybe get Mablee Normandy.
She'll know what to do.
Have we any proof?
The camp is over there.
I would not have thought it. For that
I would have my wings washed.
Damn
those murdering Glandelinian
soldiers.
What is going on down there?
Let's go and see.
What's the matter?
Am I seeing things down there?
You sure are, Joice.
We will.
How are we going to find out
who they are?
. . . we should do something
ANYTHING about this . . .
What do you see my friends,
wow.
A sign. Picnic food. They must be able
to eat.
I can't just say it, oh, it
is horrible.
Where's the camp?
Over to the rear.
Let's destroy their camp for this.
I'm getting out of here.

How horrible. I'll tell the
Blengins.

Violet sings:

O, River Aronburg's
Run runs runs runs
& has its source from
Lake Zannagustapolier.

O, River Angelina Run
Runs & runs & runs
& has her limpid source
from Lake Prostentiateneha,
O, O, and O.

The hero speaks a prayer.
Primmaradia. Primanadia or
Mangaloo Crater.
Holds up a cup.
Vanishes.

Weather reports untrue;
went to mass; no tantrums.

~

General Vivian appears. A wonderful uniform
other generals, also wonderful uniforms.
Sunday, January 5, 1969. A few bad words at god
because of an unexpected fall
at bottom of steps.
Two masses and communion.
A few tantrums in the morning

one in afternoon.
Life history.

General Vivian. It is all on account of that
Darger and his old picture.

Bitterness fills the room.

I wonder how it could be recovered. He at once
goes to General Darger's headquarters and
requests some means for the recovery of the
picture.
How am I going to recover it, your excellency?
said General Darger sadly. I have tried
various means, invading the Glandelinian
Public Libraries, and so on, but without
success.
As it is fair in war I would have ceased
(a sign appears: seized)
the book of newspapers the picture was in,
but I could not trace it though I examined
book after book. It was in some date
of either June 1911 or 1912.

June 1911 or 1912? General Vivian, sharply
and with ardent suspicion.
I thought you received the picture from her
waist?

I did but I lost it. I had received another
in a newspaper that told of the tragedy,
which was also stolen with many others
I had.
General Phelan, an

Angelinian traitor, had
something to do with the murder and
feared that I would expose him so
no doubt
?
he stole the picture so no evidence
could be made against him.

Viviana. Ahem, a traitor, hey? Well,
I'll be bound.
He must be captured at all costs.
What Glandelinian army is he in?

A division of Raymond Richmond Federal's army,
your excellency.
He goes under the name of Tamerlincia,
but that is not his name at all. He is
one of the worst men next to
Thomas and Raymond Richmond Federal.

Could you describe the murder?

Yes, your excellency. I was then a Glandelinian
child labor boss, but much against my will
as I was compelled.
Federal governed all the slave houses
in Calverina, and Phelan was his mayor.
When the Child Labor Revolution
broke out,
this little girl was elected a leader
by the child rebels and
by her gallantry
she made rapid progress, which
enraged Phelan

who got permission from Federal
to murder her

to murder her in cold blood.

I was witness to the most blood-curdling
crime ever committed in Calverina.

~

Annie Aronburg, habited in her nighties,
had been probably
occupying her mind for some time
by planning for victory
when the brute
seized her by the hair
which was loose
and flourished a razor about her face
instantly
he began to choke her,
tearing her nightie to tatters

then with one sweep of his muscular arm
he nearly severed her chest open with his razor . . .
I tried my best to stop him
but a
struggle with such a
furious giant was useless and
he got away after trying to shoot
me dead.

A Blengin appears. Please return
this book to its proper owner.
This means you, Henry D.

The Vivians appear and speak for him.
Now to go back to my ill nature
and character. I did not and will
not bear things going wrong. I
won't stand for the slightest pain
anywhere, though most of my
pains were very severe

and

I want everything

(under any conditions) to

come my way

If things

went wrong

during any kind of work I do,
I'll say
I lose my temper terribly
and
say things the saints and all the angels
would be ashamed of me for

. . .

At Jennie Richee . . .
They are lost in the wilderness
in the dark

I would not have thought
of it.

I should have had my wing
washed.

Back to the dreadful story
of Annie Aronburg.
He
got away after trying to shoot
me. I called the police,
secured the picture for special use,
and went off
to report the deed to
Calverian christian committees.
Not long after,
I lost both pictures,
one after the other . . .

I and
the little girl

had been great friends

and I
longed for the picture

as a memory of her.

General Viviana, hotly. How then
is it that the loss of the photographs
of the plain picture
also
is responsible for the situation of this war
?
General

Darger. This
is a mystery, your excellency, even to me

. . .

Are you a Christian or just serving in my
army for revenge?
I'm a perfect Angelinian and nothing
else and have no love for the enemy
of my country.

Answered Darger.
I belong to St. Anthony Parish.

Do you pray for the return of the stolen
picture?

I have offered a petition for its return . . .
I
have only done this last March,
however . . .

Saluting, General Darger withdraws
with a
better hope
than he ever had before.

~

Appearances of the Ghost of Annie Aronburg
to Darger. Please
return this book
to its proper place. This
means you, Henry D.

Someone does something.

Quietness.

It (the first appearance of the ghost)
was just
as
I reached Jennie's bridge, near Marcusian,
I was suddenly aware of a
person
following me.

I had a great dread of the Glandelinian
soldiery, so

drawing my pistol I suddenly wheeled
upon my follower;

I beheld the very likeness of the one
in the picture I had lost:

My name is Annie Aronburg.
Couldn't you
for my sake withdraw the curse
on the christians because of your
loss?

Being aroused I said.
Don't talk to me like that,
and
attempted to seize her to give her
a shaking up,
but no one was there.

As a large tree was standing, just a foot from me,
I quickly ran around it,
expecting that she had darted behind
it, but she was not there.
She was gone!
My, didn't I feel queer?

(The second appearance of the ghost)
At Phelantonburg
after being pursued by the
Glandelinians, and then by the
Abbeinians, who mistook me
for a Glandelinian soldier
on account of my gray uniform,
I escaped
them both.

Thirty or forty feet from the McHollester River
when
the same little girl, dressed all
white with hands outstretched tward
me pleadingly and
swaying
back and forth
light as a breeze, her
curly yellow hair looking yet more yellow in the afternoon
sun

when I came pretty close,
I dismounted

Don't you dare to touch me, you
friend of the Glandelinians

Screams. You refused my request, and
and yet by making you
follow me,
I saved your life. From where you
first stood, a mine had been
exploded by your would-be friends.

After this occurrence I continued my
work, and though I soon
forgot about her, I was more
determined than ever to recover her
picture,
or one just like it.

(The third appearance of the ghost)

Watching the onslaught of the
Concentinian calvary.
Against the Omarians at
McWhirter Run

I had been riding tward
McWhirter Run.
When
I heard her call me, though
however

her voice seemed far away and weak.
In
looking tward the placid waters of the
river, I thought sure
I
saw the beautiful child in the water
with

lily pads all around her;

Was it really the child's spirit persistent in her
request?

My answer. My child, I
realize now my mistake, in being
harsh to you. But I swear
before god
that I have one way to
grant your request, and that I
will tell you,
and do,
if you will reveal to me why
you appear to me and
disappear in such
a
mysterious
fashion.

She looks at him.

I told you before who I am. I am
Annie Aronburg. I was cruelly murdered
by Raymond Richardson Federal
because I was a leader
of the rebel children
who
rebelled against our
masters to gain our
freedom from slavery and misery.

As you was the one
who

had secured my picture,
and many other articles
belonging to me,
I had trust that as you
alone
have the situation of both sides
in your power,
I decided to appeal
to you
to avenge my assassination,
or the poor
Vivian girls

Chorus. The poor Vivian girls
will
will have to die for me to save their
nation and father's armies
from complete ruin and
defeat at the hands of their
Glandelinian enemies.
You
refused my request
until
I appealed a
second time, and this
is the time. If you
refuse
this time,
all
will be lost, for the foe will be victorious.

(The fourth appearance of the murdered child)

At Aronburg's Run was the last
attired as a celestial

princess, only
appearing a moment,

smiled at me, and then

was gone.
I haven't seen her since.
But now I have
joined the christian armies,
am an officer, and
have been leading one of the fiercest
charges
at Logan Zoe Rae Run . . .

Quiet, of a sudden.

Someone does something.

Once in school for some kind of cutting up,
a teacher boxed my ears,
and my father had to pay
the doctor bill for what I
did to her.

I
slashed her on the face and arm
with my long knife.

I must also say
when I was aroused
I was dangerous.
At least
when going to school
after that
my father would not let me

take my knife,
or any other weapon
with me.

Outside of that it was all right.

But I was expelled from that school
for doing that, yet if I could when
a boy I would severely revenge
punishments whether I deserved them
or not. Some boy once accused me
of stealing his wagon, which I did
not.
If I would have, I really had no
place to hide it. He hit me on the nose
with the palm of his hand. For
what I did to him in return he was
in a hospital for a long time. His parents
could do nothing against me or make
my father pay any bill because
witnesses said and was able to
prove that he and his gang of
followers ganged up on me, twelve
against one.

. . .

Somebody did steal his wagon, but
not I. What good could it be to
have stolen his darn wagon when
as I wrote before I had no place
to hide it?
If I had brought it into the house,
my father would find out who it
belonged to and make me give it
back. And punish me for stealing

it. As I had no place to hide it
I could have fully proved that I
never took it, but they still would
not believe me. So I was slammed
on the nose, and I believe I nearly
killed him.

I was a very dangerous kid if not
left alone.
My two losses have been very serious,
but the loss of the Aronburg picture
has been the greatest, has
caused the frightful
disasters
during the battles, the torment
of the Vivian girls, and the
frightful fury of the great war.
Went to mass; no tantrums.

Violet,
Mary,
Joice,
Jennie Francio,
Catherine Cecilia,
Hettie,
Annie,
Daisy Gertrude,
&
Evangelina Celestina.

Primmaradia. Primanadia or
Mangaloo Crater.
A twister called "Sweetie Pie" and the
terrible harm it did.

Storms distance approach
Danger in—squall (tropical)
The boy and girl are trying to
awaken little Vivian girl
princess sound asleep
while reclining on rock.
Flowering blossom is called
Castenallea fruit. Plant
similar to cantaloupe
when full. Please
return this book
to its proper place.
This means you, Henry D.

How horrible. I'll tell
the Blengins. I'll tell
the Blengins.
I'll tell the Blengins.

Violet sings:

Perhaps the
Blengiglomenean serpent
Perhaps the
Blengiglomenean creature
will save the little girl;

Perhaps the Perhaps the
Blengins will rest;
the Blengins will play
in the shade.

Perhaps the Grimecian
Gazoonian, perhaps

The poisonous Blengin,
Perhaps the poisonous

Blengiglomenean, a
very poisonous Blengin
of Calverina, perhaps the

Perhaps the
Perhaps the

Will save the little girl and
rest to play another day;
the Blengins will play
in the shade;

or two spangled Blengins,
or Blengins more strange
than they;

Blengiglomenean creatures,
Blengiglomenean serpents;

Perhaps the
Perhaps the

Or in their little girl form
with rams' horns
coiling out of their heads
their little round head,
like hyacinthine curls.

Perhaps the
Perhaps the

~

Vivian girls. They stand there.
With the well-cut and delicately closed
mouth;

which looked as if
it always had been
shut upon secrets.

. . .

And make a sketch of the Vivian girls as
he imagined they looked, he
found himself saying
over and over
again.

. . .

Penrod, after some considerable thoughts,
believed he could make a sketch
of the faces of the Vivian girls, and
also their father's, which he
would show General Greatheart
that he knew and could at least
that he
that could at least recognize
at least Emperor Vivian.

He rises up.
He jumps from his cot.
And
goes to a small table
near the window.

Draws from his drawer a
pencil,
and a tablet of writing paper
without lines.

Blizzard outside, and the wind was
occasionally
blowing great quantities of snow
against the windowpane,
and
the
blinding snow
sheet outside
hiding objects for a hundred feet
made it lighter.

Thirty minutes. The face of Emperor Vivian
five or six sketches of the Vivian girls.
Very unsatisfactory.
Tore them up.

Again and again. Tore them up.
Tore them up, darn it.

~

. . .

Silence. Pause. Silence.

. . .

Darn it.

~

. . .

The hasty sketching would not matter
to Penrod
if he could catch their

. . .

look . . .

but something more important.

Often he got the marked aristocratic
features or outlines of features, which
he knew absolutely were not there.

Any ordinary persons, who
have a less pronounced profile,
would have been, to
Penrod's idea,

less and more easy to draw or sketch.

And he did his best
to recall to his mind
every detail of them
which had come so often to his memory
through its well-trained habit.

. . .

Soon, to his relief, he observed that he
was drawing the likeness to a
clearer point but gradually.
And it was not long
before
the

Features were clear enough to
strike him
surely.

AS WELL DONE.
and also that of Emperor Vivian

He draws a sigh of satisfaction.

Penrod sighs, does not think
of putting on his overcoat
despite the storm outside.

Sees his boy scout approaching

The rattlesnake boy says. This is surely
a gift from God himself. It is the best gift
of all. And it proves that it is absolutely
true that your mind has done good and
perfect training.

The more you draw, the better you'll be able
to draw. Do the best you can, and draw
everything you can.

~

PART 2: CARPETS

Saturday January 4, 1969. Plenty of tantrums all
day three morning masses. One afternoon one.
Life history.

The Hero appears as Evans, a dashing
Man.

It is now seen,
after their many attempts,
that
there was an impossibility of ever
capturing Violet and her sisters alive
as long as
Evans was with them.

A moment of puzzlement;
brief tantrum.

~

Six carpets, all neatly rolled up.

Pause.

Silence.

Pause.
The carpets go on being carpets.

~

Once, however, the little girls had been
captured,
and though
unsuccessful in escaping twice
They finally succeeded
a third time:

The Glandelinians, who had made prisoners
of us,

at Phelantonburg Run,
had ordered us to roll up six rugs
so that
the soldiers could take them out.

Looking closely at the rugs
we believed
that
we immediately saw our chance to get
away
by rolling up the rugs in a way
to leave a good sized hollow in the roll,
in which each one of us could hide.

But the rugs being heavy ones,
was increased immensely by the weight
of I
and my sisters,
so that the Glandelinians
who were to take the rugs out
had all they could do
to carry them
with us in them . . .

. . .

The man carrying the rug I
was concealed in
slipped
at the head of the stairway
and he fell
the rug
suddenly
unrolled
precipitating

me
down the
stairs
so violently
that
though
fortunately
I was not
hurt,
nevertheless . . .

Something quiet happens.

Pause. Silence. Pause.

A Blengin examines her
wing. I should have had my wing

washed. Another.
They always do that.

Saturday January 28 to Thursday September 11 the
long siege of illness from the leg and left
hip from being bumped by an auto
whose driver
turned the
corner without
stopping at
Stop sign. Stopped.
What will it be?

. . .

Nevertheless the
precipitation

of my quick flight
down the
stairs
backwards
and every
form
of rolling
made me
see it
seemed a
thrillion
stars and
planits
of all colors.

I
literally went
down
most of the
way
head first
and the
Glandelinians
carrying the
other
heavier
rugs suspected
the cause
of their great
weight
when they saw
me go down
those steps

in such a
hurry.

And my sisters were at once seized.

The officer at the lower room.
Trying to escape, eh? You little brat
Well you just come right down to
the first floor where we can watch
you.

They watch her.

Silence.

Pause.

Silence.

. . .

Bad fall, pain in head, aggrieved.
Say, Colonel Frank Francis, do you
think anyone could come down
any faster than I did?

I
and my sisters
were brought down into the
officers' quarters,
and
one of the soldiers told
of our attempts to escape, and
how
one of us

had been accidentally
dumped
down the steps
by Private Henry Darger,
who was carrying the rug
!

. . .

Who was carrying the rug
concealing me.

A rug unrolls. Unscrolls. Reveals

A picture. Psst.

Don't worry. We Blengins
will help you escape.

The officers laugh at Private Henry
Darger.
Little girls will do anything
to escape.

I guess you would, says Evans.
Your daring escapes, and attempts
to escape, have made my hair raise on
end
at times. What you
little girls do
would make me shiver with fright.

Music. We notice a dark dark cloud an oval

off to the right of the

~

At Jennie Richee
During full fury of the storm they escape

~

At Jennie Richee
Storm distance approach
Danger in—squall (tropical)
The boy and girls are trying
to awaken little Vivian girl
princess sound asleep
while reclining on rock.
Flowering blossom is called
Castanallea fruit. Plant
similar to cantaloupe
when full.

~

At Jennie Richee
Out in the open they view the approaching
storm (Blengins are the ones with horns).

~

At Jennie Richee
They have the suspicion of bad tropical storm
approaching.

~

At Jennie Richee
Racing through a field of gigantic flowers
to seek shelter as the storm renews.

~

At Jennie Richee
They mingle with the child prisoners in the

absence of guards they overcome to get
them to quit work and follow them next
morning.

~

At Jennie Richee
Next morning child prisoners flee across
Aronburg Run River. Little Vivians on bank
right of picture try to get them to turn back
before running into trap.

~

At Jennie Richee
Harassed by unseen foe as storm approaches
terrified kids hide behind bushes while
the little Vivians defiant by remaining
in the open.

~

At Jennie Richee
Cross river by swimming and beat escaping
pursuers. Land on North side and notice
height of tropical plants.

~

Burning the crazy images tossed in all
directions by the explosion. Boy hit on
the head by one of them is doctored in
next picture.

~

Let's take him to a doctor. That thing
hit him hard.
This is not a surprise.

Not playing. This is the real thing.
He is a midget doctor.
We can burn those
crazy images over
there.
Sign. Picture no two from
other side.

~

At Calmanrina
Almost engulfed by opposing soldiers of both
sides during hand-to-hand fight they succeed in
escaping by climbing a tall tree in the
region of battle.

~

At Jennie Richee
All are seized by pursuing Glandelinian soldiers
three hours later.

~

At Jennie Richee
They are seized by Glandelinians with
dogs.
Glandelinians. There they go.
Vivians. I once hit General Manley with a stone and I am
afraid of the enemy ever since.
What or who is after you that scares
you so?
I do not know what is the matter. She
was running like mad every time I see
her and one looks so scared and yet
angry.

Hurry, everyone. Don't stand there talking.
They're coming very fast with dogs.

~

See my wing? What if I tapped you
with it? I could have injured you
badly. You done wisely to stop. I
saw you always running like crazy.
Will you explain why? Anyone after
you?

~

Who owns this? (A birdhouse)
Aw don't be such a little mouse and
put your hands around from your
face. Nothing will happen to you.
You said a mouthful.
I second the motion.

~

Yeah, darn it.
What is going on down there, Nancy?*
Let's maybe get Mablee Normandy. She'll
know what to do.
Some kids have been cut over there.
Have any proof?
This is the knife they used.
The camp is over there.
Make them who done it give up to us
or destroy them all.
*Glandelinian soldiers committed a total
murder of children.
They always do that.

And how.
I feel something's happened.
I would not og it. For that I would have
my wings washed.
Damn those murdering Glandelinian solders.
What's wrong?
Call that all fair in war? That's first-degree
murder. It's cruel. Look what I'm holding
(A severed head) and this is no image but the head
of a real child.
I wish I had those gray-coated devils who did
that. I'd pray they are baseballs and my
wings are baseball bats.
I feel like a baby to know those murderous Glandelinians
could do that.
Do the same to them.
What is going on down there?
Let's go and see.
What's the matter?
What do you see, my friends? Wow.
What's the matter?
Am I seeing things down there?
You sure are, Nancy.
(Picnic food. They must be able to eat.)
I just can't say it, oh, it is horrible.
Where's the camp?
Over to the rear.
Let's destroy their camp for this.
We will.
How are we going to find out who they are?
Couldn't we do something about this?
I'm getting out of here.
How horrible. I'll tell the Blengins.*
Sure? What do you think?

What do you think when the Glendelinians
do this to innocent kids?
A cloaked man.
Primmaradia. Primanadia or
Mangaloo Crater.
How horrible. I'll tell the Blengins.

I'll tell the Blengins.
I'll tell the Blengins.
I'll tell the Blengins.

Violet sings:

O, River Aronburg's
Run runs runs runs
& has its source from
Lake Zannagustapolier.

O, River Angelina Run
Runs & runs & runs
& has her limpid source
from Lake Prostentiateneha
O, O, and O

~

PART 3: CAVERNS

Lost in a cavern

darkness visible.

An old man, coughing, shuffles about.

Pause. Silence. Pause.

If I had known at the time
of the cause
of my being sent to that
children's nuthouse, I surely would have
never forgiven
those at the
Mercy of Our Lady Home
and would have
revenged it the very first
chance I had.

I a feeble-minded kid!

I knew more than the whole shebang
in that place

I was then called crazy.
I had I believe more brains than all
combined. None of them I found
ever even knew geography or
history. I did. My spelling, figures,
and reading and writing was more
excellent than theirs.
My finding it out there are many
cities in this country and the old world
they could not spell or pronounce
I could
Berlin and Dresden are still the most
beautiful cities in the world.
Berlin is the largest next to London and
New York City
February 20 Friday 1970 Same from 1969

Till now. Many days of bad tember same
work daily mass communion and walks
eating Jalooka fruit before its ripe.

~

Primmaradia. Primanadia or
Mangaloo Crater.

Heavy de horse radish.

He hums a song.

As I said before, I received admonition
from Sister Rose because of my

. . .

enforced left-handedness, until
I could prove it was impossible
with my right hand.

Once

In searching for something that
got lost from me
in a very dark place,
an
enclosure of the out exit

on the ground floor
behind the dining room,
by which you go outside
by the rear

I scared some young woman
(she was cowardly and timid anyhow)
out of her wits accidentally.

When Sister Rose heard of it
by someone telling her, she scolded me
good, and said she believed that
I am really crazy.

Silence.

Pause.

Silence.

Brief flash of a solitary Blengin washing
her wing.

Somewhere someone does something.

While working at St. Joseph Hospital
and then at the Alexian Hospital, I
got on me a very mean streak
because of prayers not being answered
and a question over snow.

Before this happened, I was a
daily attendant at Mass and Holy
Communion.

Then foolishly and very sinfully
I stopped going to Mass and Holy
Communion, and when work
was unusually heavy
at both places I badly sang awfully
blasphemous words at God for hours
without stopping
I am surprised that for the words
I sang God did not strike me.
But no he did not.
I believe he knew

. . .

there was a time coming
when I would wisely change my
ways.
It did happen. It was while
I was working in the
bandage room.
Up there were days
when the work was so scarce that
I almost had nothing to do.

In some sort of a magazine
I read of a young fellow
who
when losing his fortune he
turned bandit and robbed
and killed at will.

He was betrayed by false women
friends arrested and being found
guilty at his trial was condemned
to be hanged.

When he died he went to hell and
was tormented horribly by fiends.

There was not only descriptions
of the story but as many pictures.
The pictures of his torments in the
fires of hell, and by the demons
scared me into repentance
and I stayed good and after
confession have been going to
daily Mass and confession frequently
and also Holy Communion ever since.

~

Guard those timid kids from any
more danger. Those prisoners
might escape again.
The trial is delayed. Too bad.

~

Awful slow getting the trial started.

~

At Jennie Richee
Two days later captured again

~

Hurry with those darn kid
prisoners. Into the stockade.
What's keeping you, Mike?
Hurry please
Sixty-three kids listed here who and
what nine kids are nuded and
why.

Child slaves maybe.
What's your hurry?
Hold your horses [Mike]

~

The trial [Sign]
will begin [Sign]
in three minutes [Sign]
. . . afraid of . . .
What's wrong now?

~

Here. Put this on, scardy.
Scardy? Don't make fun
of me.
At Jennie Richee
Who does this belong to?
I would not want to be in
their place [Sign]
Their trial begins at two
o'clock [Sign]
They will plead not
guilty [Sign]

~

Hard-pressed during attack by
pursuing enemy they become
lost in cavern of volcanic
Mount Soutuumia . . . or
Primmaradia or Primanadia or
Mangaloo Crater.

~

January 1 1971 and also 1st of February
1971. From Friday 1970 till Monday
1971. Everything I did was the same.
Including writing a fictional story of
a huge huge twister called "Sweetie Pie"
and the unbelievable horror it did.

. . .

From February 1971 to December 1971
Not much history until October when
I had an eye operation of the left one
because of a serious infection and was
in bed and unstill a little before Christmas
because I couldn't because of an
unusual eye covering for protection
placed by the doctor. I had a poor a
very poor nothing like Christmas.
Never had a good Christmas all my life
nor a good new good new year and
now reviewing it I am very bitter but
. . . not resentful as I feel I should . . .

I do wish I could be back
working there again.
To make matters worse I am an artist
and
cannot hardly stand on
my feet because of
my knee to paint on the
top of the long picture.

Went to mass; no tantrums.
!

. . .

Now I am walking the streets and
again going to Mass as usual what
will it be for New Year's 1972 1972
God only knows this year was a
very bad one Hope not to repeat
if so—

New Year's Resolution: I'll do the same
next year as I did this year
and that is final.

January 1 1972—to January 1973
What will it be?

Violet sings:

O, River Aronburg's
Run runs runs runs
& has its source from
Lake Zannagustapolier.

O, River Angelina Run
Runs & runs & runs
& has her limpid source
from Lake Prostentiateneha
O, O, and O.

~

Primmaradia. Primanadia or
Mangaloo Crater.

~

At Jennie Richee
Hard-pressed during storm by pursuing

enemy they become lost in cavern of
volcanic Mt. Soutuumnia.

~

A picture.
The Way Out.

~

Another.
Three fairy-winged Tuskerhorians.

~

Another.
Young Striped Blengin.

~

Another.
They admire the beauty of Tropical nimbus
clouds.

~

Another two pictures.
Gazook; and Grimecian Gazoonian.

~

Another.
Lost in volcanic caverns.

~

And another.
Odalisque; In the garden.

~

A Jennie.
A nouveau, la fuite.

Silence.

Pause.

Silence.

~

Another picture.
Sacred Heart; Explosion.

~

Another.
Everything is all right.

~

Another.
Flowers and girls in polka-dot dresses.

~

A last picture.
The Blengins play under shelter.

~

Violet sings:

At Jennie Richee
What if I tapped
you with my wing?
What if I hurt
you badly, sadly?
Who would help you?
Who would help you
escape the trap?
What will it be?

What will it be?
O, it all would
end badly, sadly
at Jennie Richee
What will it be?
What will it be?

Someone does something.

(Millstones, not feathers.)

Silence. Pause. Silence.

End of play.

Antigone

. . . and on the roof of my head . . .

—MAZZY STAR

Antigone was first presented in 2000 by Big Dance Theater under the direction of Paul Lazar and with choreography of Annie-B Parson at Classic Stage Company, and in 2002 at Dance Theater Workshop.

PERSONS OF THE PLAY

All parts are played by the THREE FATES, also THREE FACTS, on their way to becoming the THREE GRACES; with the exception of !Ǝ. THE SHRIEK OPERATOR (pronounced "E shriek"), an unknown god of unknown origin who is named for the special symbol of logical notation as described in the appendix of *The Cambridge Dictionary of Philosophy* (1999 edition). The traditional parts are CREON, ISMENE (ANTIGONE's sister), CREON's son, HAEMON (ANTIGONE's betrothed), CREON's wife, EURYDICE (in my version also the prophet, TEIRESIAS), and a CHORUS of Theban citizens.

PART 1 [●]

Once, at the beginning of time, the three Fates, unpleasant young girls, enacted the story that was to become that of Antigone. The three girls played all the parts with hats instead of masks, and a whole rack of customary costumery.

A battlefield. Heaps of dead clothing. Dead clothing strewn all over. Three girls watch from a distance. Unknown god as a bodiless shadow approaches. As a swirl of fabric. I am the Shriek Operator. !Ǝ. I am the unique situation. I am the uncanny and have come to this place, place crowded with corpses and the stench of death. I am the Shriek Operator and am very pleased with all this slaughter, this horror, this misfortune. Misfortune out of contrast, sprung hinges, what creaks, what is fundamentally broken. Sand pours without anyone willing it. Pours from above. From the sky. Something is covered. Something mangled and horribly dead. Pours. Horripilation. Who. Who did this? I am and I am not named Antigone, daughter of a man whose name. The one of whom it is said, he possessed one eye too many. Saw too much. Learned too little from what he saw. Incurious. Curious, how incurious. Mind made up. Driven from place to place by !Ǝ. The Shriek Operator. The shorthand for "... there exists a unique situation...." The shorthand that stands in total contradistinction to the shorthand for "It will always be that." Shorthand for "It always was that."

A song: Thus, it always was / thus it will always be that / thus, if I am named / who I think I am / I will always be caught in the terrible terrible / cat's cradle. For I / / both must and must not / bury my dead brother, / Polyneices.

A Chorus: Of all things strange, humankind / is the most strange. / The cat's cradle / is news to the spider, / for all things go round and round; for / I was a stranger and you took me in; for / I was a stranger and you took me not in; for / / straw, straw, straw, / straw shows which way the wind blows, / and an empty belly thinks the moon is green cheese; for / / (the King of Spiders) / / Up he was stuck /up he was stuck /up he was stuck / and in the very upness / of his stuckitude / he fell. / / (Straw, straw, straw, straw.) / / And what I learned from my long / life of spinning string, /life of measuring string, / life of snip, snip, snip: / / You can't beat something with nothing.

Creon watches her. I wonder what she is. Doing in her thinking. He says: The rule is: Eteocles, hero. Polyneices, the logical opposite: traitor. If one, then not the other. This is an unanalyzable truth. Truth is true. (That is why it is called the truth.) A rupture. Time backs up and shakes itself like a wet dog.

I am a stranger, Ismene, my eyes see the clearest. I'm clearing out. As she goes: Devil take the hindmost. Antigone. A hint's as good as a kick. Take the double-faced mask (that they were wearing). I see so clear I don't need one. What I need is a good hat. A fatal hat. She puts one on. She carefully balances an egg on one end.

Three Fates dance the Dance of Hollow Time and Hollow Earth. Everything hollow with a hole in it. Earth and sky. Ocean and the Vast, electromagnetic carpets of stars and eggs and all possible hats. Celestial eggs. Egg egg egg. Most eggs are electrical in some way. Most aren't. Let's turn her in. Who? Antigone. Let's turn her inside out. See what god. You can't carry an egg in two baskets. You can't be in the same place at the same time. You simply can't.

She did it. Creon, she. Did what? You know. The bad thing, at the bad place. She buried him, or tried to.

A Chorus: Let us invoke / the rupture of silence in the hollow of uncanniness. / / Let us invoke / the pause before the rupture of the already known in / the presence of the already dead. / / (Gods love to collect at the place of the dead as though it were a compass focus.) / / Let us invoke / the arrival of the gods and the dissolution of all / that is merely human. / / Let us invoke the pause before the silence before all of this; / for earth, hollow earth, / / (hollow, hollow, hollow) / / is the house of the dead, and the place / of engendering. The branching of facts, / facts which are opposed, contradictory. / Dog and cat facts. / / Let us invoke / the howl before the primordial howl. Let us invoke / the spider that taught the spider, the / very first one, / / how to be a spider. / How to creep. / (And be creepy.) They all do the spider. They all howl. They all creep.

A Chorus: Humankind is the most terrible, / / the most terrible of all things. / For / when you step on your own head / it is time to go home, and harmony / seldom makes a headline. / Some wheelbarrows are red, but / all insects have antennae / for the name of an actual world is pronounced "a round" / once you allow the Facts to slide. / / (Slide, slide, slide.) / / All down the slope to chaos will glide / and what is not yet hidden / will learn to hide, hide, hide / and to abide. / / (Hide, hide, hide.) / / There on that slippery slope / of the terrible unbidden, oh / that I had in the wilderness of logic / a place for wayfaring men. / Those / / who mind the difference between / things that are, and things that are not / things that are, and things that are not / things that are, and things that are not. / / Hold on Antigone, hold on. / Abide, you bride of silence. Abide. / / Coda: / Save soap and waste paper. / Two pizzas for one low price.

Creon as Antigone arrests Antigone who is Creon. A confusion arises. Someone does something. All change hats. Nothing feels right.

PART 2 [RED FOX]

This includes what is buried. Harvest, ingathered by lightning, in view of all. This was done by Antigone, her, a bride of quietness, one of the *symparanekromenoi,* one of the living dead.

Verdict. Interment in the house of death, while yet alive. Agon. Antigone. In her geode.

Chorus of ordinary citizens. Well.... Eleven don't make a dozen. Give 'em an ell and they'll take a mile. The end of the thief is the gallows. The end crowns the work. The heavy end of the match is the light end. Ask the spider. She knows. They fall silent and dance the Dance of Charm and Distance. Silence. Pause. Distance. They dance the Dance no one has ever. They dance the Dance of Withdrawal. They dance a nothing dance. !Ǝ. The Shriek Operator appears. The hidden takes them all, perhaps. (...there exists a unique situation...) Teiresias (played by Eurydice) appears. He is a man and sometimes not. Creon

Your offerings have been rejected. Creon: I do not have much information on this except the general statement of the Agency that there is nothing in the files to disprove her (Antigone's) communist connections. [This is not a comment on communism; it is an instance of logical error.] Okay. Okay. Eteocles, hero. Polyneices, traitor. That's simple enough. The news is what has been forgotten. The mystery. The absolute. The uncanny. The unanalyzable, Creon. The unanalyzable. Big words no one understands, or pretends not to. A little hole will sink a ship. A big old ship. A hole is nothing at all, but you can break your neck in it. No one can dig up a hole. Wisdom doesn't always speak Greek. The unseen, too. The incomprehensible. A wise man sees twice as much as he talks about. If things were to be done twice, all would be wise. Just let things rock along.

Haemon watches Antigone as she watches Creon. Fell in love with her violet eye. She thinks. Do the thing and have done with it. Teiresias turns on Creon. Creon turns on Haemon. Haemon turns on Antigone. Pause. Silence. Pause. Antigone turns on Creon, as the whirlwind watches from out of the cat's cradle. She says. Someone is always watching someone else, Creon. Someone is always overhearing. Why must this be? Each thing has a right place if you know how to place it. My brother's body, for instance. There is such a thing as motion in one place. Spirit is action. This attempted burial is re-action. You dramatize the issue. To dramatize is to think against the self. To hell with self, any self, yours or mine or another. I got my idea like you got yours. By watching another. I? A watcher? Precisely. You watched me and despise me for my clean, unpleasant spirit. I watched the burial of my brother by an unknown god. Death and crumpled paper. The true folly is the folly of burying the dead. May I go now? She goes. Fool. Fool. Teiresias goes: Those who speak truth, speak shadows. He that is not with me is against me. For every action there is a reaction. Disaster being the final logic of human action (Haemon). I don't give a damn for any damn man that don't give a damn for me.

A battlefield. Heaps of empty clothing. Dead clothing strewn all over. Two girls watch from a distance. Unknown god as a bodiless shadow approaches as a swirl of fabric. I am the Shriek Operator. !Ǝ. I am the unique situation. I am the uncanny and have slunk to this place crowded with corpses and the scent of death. I am the Shriek Operator and am very pleased by all this misfortunate contrast, this contradiction, this contraction, because I am what lies outside language and therefore cannot be understood. Cannot be understood, do you understand? You are all housed in your unhousedness. The sand that buried Polyneices poured without anyone pouring it (. . . there is the unique . . .). The unique is what is outside language and they dance the Dance of What Is Outside Language. This is a dance of nothing. All go. The earth is dark. The nothing that happens now is the force that fills what is empty. All go except for Teiresias. Who mourns in a little Dance of Error and Disclosure. He says: Polyneices lived his death above the ground. Antigone below. The hidden take us far, far from the place we know, perhaps. A chorus: He who speaks of nothing does not know / what he is doing. / / In speaking of nothing he makes it into / a something. / / In speaking he speaks against / what he intended. / He contradicts himself.

Another chorus: What is more weird than man? / What is more weird than man / and woman? / / All mastery depends on motion. / Climbing the purple hills. / Driving through the mountainous / seas. For even the purple murex / lacks the red; for / the bugle cry of what's red is the / pot calling the kettle black. / / (Kettle, kettle, kettle.) / / The hole and the patch should / be commensurate, as the / dog to his man should / be obedient. It is as if I / ask you to prove this bicycle / belongs to Hector, and you reply / "All the bicycles around here / belong to Hector"; or the / / fallacy of too many questions, the / fallacy of affirming the consequent, or the / fallacy of denying the antecedent, or the / fallacy of hasty generalization, or the / fallacy of irrelevant conclusion, or the / fallacy of misplaced concreteness, or the / fallacy of many questions, or the / fallacy of accident; or the fallacy of bad faith. / / What is more weird what is more weird / than red feather than black kettle / what is more weird.

Eurydice (played by Teiresias) walks in a slow circle. She is thinking of what to say to Creon. A part of the city has been swallowed by mud (we hope it's mud). A lahar, it is called. Is this a god's dog's doing or what? Shall the hole in the center of the world be stopped by a girl? And not by the corpse of my son who fell in love with her violet eyes. Violent eye. We already know what will happen. Why? Why must we go into the whole damn piece of crapshoot playacting if we know the dice are loaded? Time does not like this remark. Becomes a weasel, or a vicious hedgehog, backs up, puffed up in raging horripilation. Antigone is stamping her foot. Teiresias as Teiresias: What are you trying to do? The three Facts go in and out of a line like a. Like a cat's cradle. The three Fates Clotho Lachesis Atropos. I am trying to stop something by stamping my foot. Omens are over. The signlessness of the omens is the most uncanny. Terrible, terrible, terrible. I am unable to stop thinking. Thinking of how to make a curse capable of ripping through human flesh like a goldarn bullwhip. We are surrounded by omens we cannot read. Surrounded by death and crumpled paper. Newsprint we cannot read. All the print that fits the new, us, the walking dead, dead shadows. *Symparanekromenoi.*

Antigone. A witness to her own death. Thereby twice dead. A voyeur. A stranger in the house of being. Antigone: I am going to shave my belly. I am going deep into a hole. I am going to watch them. The ones who think they can watch over me. Deep in a hole and come out the other side. Place where things stand as they are. One two three. They follow her. The three Facts, each wrapped up in her own fabric. Each carries her own dumb, expensive wand. Day. Night. Death and crumpled paper. Creon and Haemon are unable to speak to each other. Circle and stare. Watchers watched. Night says no to day. Silence.

Pause. A small unpleasant animal crosses the vast emptiness of infinite spaces. They watch this. Not a very nice animal, in fact.

Silence.

We behold, for the first time, the curvature of the earth. Someone looks out and holds an egg. If X, then Y. Logic, someone says. A song: Thus it will always be / thus it will always be / thus it will always be; / kettle, kettle, kettle, / boil up a fragrant tea for me. / On the day of my final day / on the anniversary of me. / The fatal anniversary of me. / / Looks around, shivering and afraid. Look at her (this is a command). Alone and cold. No one to love her. No one to protect her. Nothing but stillness. Stillness laying waste. The laying waste of stillness. Now she is the focal point of stillness. And

and

and

and the gods are coming. Unknown ones and the unseen.

Collision of the necessary and insoluble in her girl's face. Each Fact denies another. All change hats. Nothing works. Nothing works, and the Rock emerges from the gloom. Castle Rock. In the middle of air. High above us. What is closed begins to open. Something catches us by surprise. It is Haemon, falling upon his sword, as is the tragic fashion. We hear his death agony. Slow way to die. Time passes unconcerned. His death is horrible. We watch him from a distance (this is a command). We feel nothing for him. We feel nothing human. We feel cold and alone. Antigone looks at us. We look at Antigone. Nothing moves us. Nothing moves Antigone. This is the cat's cradle. We feel nothing because we are no longer what's called "human."

A song: The devil wipes his tail with Creon's pride. / Listen to Little Jack fry up an eyeball for an egg. / Bubba tubba bubba tubba bubba tubba bup. / / I am the kind of girl tired of always being wise. / I am the tin can tied to my own damn tail. / / Fry up an eyeball for an egg. / Leg up, leg down, leg up, leg down. / Egg, egg, egg, egg, stupid old egg. / / Oedipus, he had one eye too many perhaps. / / Quietly, one of the three: I am the tin can tied to my own damn tail. Slow fade to black in which we hear them sing the song over again till they get it right. More right. Over and over. Silence.

Pause. In which Time becomes a one-legged crow. Crow on a withered bough. Crow having a hard time cleaning her wing.

Silence.

One senses the presence of an unknown god. Then another. Then another. We behold for the first time (once more) the curvature of the earth. Once more the Rock appears. Castle Rock. In the middle of air. High above us. The Rock opens. A brilliant geode, violet and luminous. Antigone is enshrined within. She looks almost like a goddess. Which one? No man can say. No man can say. No man can say. How many can stay. And I slipped out the back and I made myself very small and I slipped out the back way and when I awoke. I was in a different place, a thin place, as though it were the place of a compass focus. And the lines of force radiated out from my heart in all directions and I could feel these lines of force as though I were a god and not merely a nasty girl, a girl tired of being the wise one. Radiated out from my still beating heart

•

And I traveled to the center of the world and I made wicked-awful charms and devised ghastly rituals, and some of these are for the propitiation of unknown gods. Unseen gods. Gods both unknowable and unseeable. For what lies buried in the center of the world are the last words of the barely alive but just about to be dead: Lord help my poor soul. / Jesu. / Give it (a candle) to me; it is time now. / Peace, peace, peace. / . . . Addio, Mamma mia, addio, Mamma mia. / Edith. / It is very beautiful , but I want to go farther away. / I am not worthy. / Fire. / Moderately. I am continuing to orbit. / Death today, 66. / It is time. . . . Ay, Jesus. / Let not poor Nelly starve. / I want to go there. / Always. Always water for me. / Thank you, doctor. / Doro, I can't get my breath. / Well, if it must be so. / I am better now. / Don't give up the ship. Blow her up. / I have a terrible headache. / May God never abandon me. / Get my swan "costume" ready. / I shall be glad to find a hole to creep out of the world at.

All now. And what lies buried below shall engender a time to come with many wonderful things. Let there be Spiders and Eggs and, and Hats, and gods. For all good things come in threes. Three Fates. Three Graces. Three blind mice. . . . Three dead Greeks. Dead Eurydice. Dead Haemon. Dead Antigone. And as I wondered, freely and threely, I thought I could see back to the old days at Thebes. She watches from within her geode. A place she calls "The Rat Minaret." Watches Creon and the Shriek Operator !Ǝ. The one torments the other. City half-buried in a tide of shit, Creon. Hey, Creon, look at me. Look at me. Creon, if it looks like shit, smells like shit, tastes like shit. . . . Hey, Creon, baby.

Look at me. Hey, I got no teeth. I'm on drugs. He plays the washboard and sings a song: I've been a sinner, I've been a scamp, / but now I'm willin' to trim my lamp, / So blow, Gabriel, blow! Oh yes, Creon, yes, yes, yes. Of course, we'll go back to Albania one day. But meanwhile we have to make a new life for ourselves at The Ritz. Whoopee! Creon flees. !Ǝ. The Shriek Operator flies after gesticulating with a meat hook.

PART 3 [RED CLOUD]

Once, at the beginning of time, the Three Fates, young girls then, enacted the story that was to become that of Antigone. The three girls played all the parts, with hats instead of masks (well, maybe one mask is allowed), and a whole rack of customary costumery.

In this way they learned their nature and the nature of things and became the three Graces. Aglaia. Thalia. Euphrosyne. The one who gives. The one who receives. The one who returns. Three Facts who are the three Fates who are the three Graces who are the three Facts. Who are the three. Who are the. Who are. Who. The Fates turn into Graces just at the precise moment, Antigone, in their enactment, turns into a flame.

After the transformation they discover a puppet Sophocles in a wooden box. Using an ear trumpet they recite the first stanza from the second stasimon, in Greek, into the puppet's ear (actually, there is no puppet, only a girl's hand enacting the puppet).

There is wonder in his eyes; but there is much they will not reveal, much that must be withheld:

> There is much that is strange, but nothing that surpasses man in strangeness . . .

Lights up. They do something with expensive, stupid wands. Strange uncanny looks and smiles. First: To be positive: To be mistaken at the top of one's voice. Second: Fish and visitors smell in three days. Third: The play is finished.

Indeed it is.

End of play.

Almost.

Repeat the whole three times so that each may play Antigone, each Creon. So that each may be a whirlwind. Repeat three times exactly the same (only different). The first repetition, being partially erased, is seven minutes long; the second, only three. Silence. Pause. Silence. The third repetition takes no time at all. Now the play is truly finished (some may not think so).

The Fez

The Fez was commissioned by the Actors Theatre of Louisville as a T-shirt play in 1998. It was read at the Little Theater at Tonic in 2002.

The Fez, *a play, begins with twenty-two minutes from the top of any of the better class of contemporary classic American or British play, a play properly inflated with moral updraft of a clear and paraphraseable kind. After the initial twenty-two minutes, Something Strange happens: the actors drop out of their roles and are astounded to find themselves on stage; some try to ignore the fact that the charmed spell of the theater has somehow absented itself; others simply flee the stage and the emptiness of its artifice in horror; still others bravely go on, although they have either forgotten how to act, or what their lines are, or both. Twenty-two dwarves drag onstage an immense ceremonial wagon (as in the engraving by Albrecht Dürer), with appropriate fanfares, drones, and chants, which continue through the end of the play. All the dwarves wear red fezzes. Atop the ceremonial wagon is a gigantic fez, also red. The dwarves begin a sequence of strange dances: they do the Muscle Beach; they do the Fur-Lined Hangover; they do the Jamaican Car Service; they do the Hokey Locus; they do the Spinal Fusion. All the remaining actors stare at this and wonder, as do the dwarves who have been planted in the audience as shills. There is a twenty-two-minute fade to black.*

The Difficulty of Crossing a Field

> *Something walks here   a little breath in hell   without its ghost.*
>
> —MURIEL RUKEYSER

The Difficulty of Crossing a Field, based on the story by Ambrose Bierce, with music by David Lang, was commissioned by Carey Perloff and the American Conservatory Theater (ACT) in San Francisco in 1994 through the National Theatre Artist Residency Program. It was first performed at ACT under the direction of Carey Perloff in 2002; the East Coast premiere was the Ridge Theater production at Montclair State University in 2006 under the direction of Bob McGrath.

PERSONS AND SETTING OF THE PLAY

ARMOUR WREN, a Selma planter, WILLIAMSON's neighbor; a PRESIDING MAGISTRATE, at the inquest regarding the strange disappearance of WILLIAMSON, a Selma planter; his wife MRS. WILLIAMSON; their daughter, THE WILLIAMSON GIRL; her friend, the BLACK BOY SAM; ANDREW, the overseer and brother of WILLIAMSON; an OLD WOMAN, also African American; VIRGINIA CREEPER; a CHORUS of slaves, field hands, and other black folk on the Williamson estate, six miles from Selma, Alabama, in July 1854; and WITNESSES at the inquest shortly thereafter.

NOTE

The occasional appearance of an asterisk in the middle of a speech indicates that the next speech begins to overlap at that point. The overlapping speeches are all clearly marked in the text.

SCENE [BELLADONNA]

The First Telling. The empty field at night. Only, the face of the moon is MRS. WILLIAMSON*'s. We hear night noises; she speaks quietly.*

MRS. WILLIAMSON:

How could I have known, back in Memphis, what I cannot tell, nor find a name for, here? I swear to you I did not see nothing. I swear, it was . . . it was . . .

A cloud passes over her face.

Gap. Gulf. Abyss. Pause.

More than a mere disappearance.
More than a mere disappearance.
More than a mere disappearance.

Pause.

I had no reason to think I had at
the time lost my mind. It was only
that I have never seen nor heard of Mister Williamson since.
Nor of Mrs. Williamson.

VIRGINIA CREEPER, THEN CHORUS OF SLAVES:

Round, Square, Juniper, Crabgrass,
Candlestick,* Limbo, Clock, Bumblebee,

Jackass, Crawdad, Nuisance, Puissance,
Doorbell, and Virginia Creeper.

MRS. WILLIAMSON:

There are more mysteries in Selma,*
There are more mysteries in Selma
in Selma, Alabama
There are more mysteries than . . . than . . .
than there are bad little girls
in the Darkman's night school

VIRGINIA CREEPER:

We are building a nation.
We are building a nation.
We are building a nation.
We are building an erasure.
An erasure of John C. Calhoun, may he rest in peace; an erasure of the Kansas–Nebraska Act of 1854, may he rest in peace; an erasure of Arrangement and regularity, which forms the great secret of doing things well, may he rest in peace. Clock, clock. Grandfather Clock. Of the tribe of Clock

MRS. WILLIAMSON:

Whirling* whirling whirling

VIRGINIA CREEPER:

But I fear his true mode of locomotion,
like that of Prince Zandor,* was more
humble: the singleton crutch, or cane.
Of the tribe of Crutch, or Cane.

CHORUS:

Prince Zandor! Ah, Prince Zandor!

MRS. WILLIAMSON:

Hey, those are people down there.

VIRGINIA CREEPER:

Wonder wonder wonder thing
Wonder what and wonder sing.

CHORUS:

Wonder wonder
Wonder wonder

MRS. WILLIAMSON:

Wonder wonder wonder thing and
Wonder what and wonder sing.
They look slightly familiar.
Hurrah. Hurray.
Wonder wonder.
Moon what, moon what—
moon what I am.
moon what I am.
Wonder what I am.

VIRGINIA CREEPER:

Wonder what I am.

THE BOY SAM:

Wonder what in heck I am.

MRS. WILLIAMSON:

Moon, moon, moon, I am naturally under the circumstances
a full moon. And the true wonder is—
Wonder what I am doing way up here.
Alone with the wonder of not knowing.
Something or someone, who like my husband, has been

caused to disappear.
A something went walking here with a crooked walking stick
to top a flower.
A flower in a field.
He was a flower. It topped him.
I wonder what has become* of what?

The MOON walks off on stilt legs.

THE BOY SAM:
Wonder who I am.
Wonder who I am.
Wonder who in heck I am.

End of First Telling.

INTERLUDE

THE WILLIAMSON GIRL:
Today is the day
Today is the day is the day
Today is the day is the day
is the day is the day is the day
is the day

SCENE [MONKSHOOD]

Second Telling. A closed room, with no windows. A MAN before us, a single light illuminating his face. This is the PRESIDING MAGISTRATE. Other men, WITNESSES, presumably, sit next to the wall. In the shadows beyond, another MAN sits at a desk. This is the Selma planter, ARMOUR WREN. There is a table to the right of the PRESIDING MAGISTRATE, and on it a piece of white cloth, perhaps a shroud, lies in disarray.

ARMOUR WREN:

I had driven some two hundred yards
beyond the point where we had encountered
him when I said to my son, James, "I
forgot to tell Mister Williamson about
those horses."

PRESIDING MAGISTRATE:

And Mister Williamson, at that point, was
in full view?

ARMOUR WREN:

Yes, I believe so. He had walked down from
his front porch, perhaps fifty yards across
the lawn between the house and the public
road or, as it was called, "the pike."

PRESIDING MAGISTRATE:

Was this the field you, and the others,
have mentioned?

ARMOUR WREN:

No, no. You see, just beyond this road
lay a close-cropped pasture of ten acres,
level and without a tree, rock, or any
natural or artificial object on its surface.
At the time I am speaking of, that morning,
there was not even a domestic animal
in the field. In another piece of land,
beyond the pasture, a dozen slaves were
at work under the overseer, Andrew.

PRESIDING MAGISTRATE:

And all of this was open and visible?

ARMOUR WREN:

All of it was open and visible.

PRESIDING MAGISTRATE:

All of it?

ARMOUR WREN:

All of it, Williamson's own brother, Andrew,
was the overseer.

PRESIDING MAGISTRATE:

This man Andrew has already given his
testimony. You may continue, Mister Wren.

ARMOUR WREN:

I do not know how to continue exactly, sir.
The event proceeded as I have described.
After driving some two hundred yards
beyond the point where we had greeted
each other—Mister Williamson and myself—
I said to James, "I forgot to tell Mister
Williamson about those horses."

CHORUS:

I forgot tell Mister Williamson about those horses.

PRESIDING MAGISTRATE:

What exactly was it you were preparing
to tell Mister Williamson concerning
those horses?

ARMOUR WREN:

That is the odd thing. For the life of me
I cannot recall.

PRESIDING MAGISTRATE:

You are very certain you cannot recall what
it was?

ARMOUR WREN:

I am very certain I cannot recall.

CHORUS:

I am very certain I cannot recall.

PRESIDING MAGISTRATE:

Well, let us go over the facts as we know
them: the horses were your horses, were
they not, Mister Wren?

ARMOUR WREN:

Yes. I had sold them to Mister Williamson,
yes. Horses, which were to be sent for that
day. But for some reason not now remembered
it would be inconvenient to deliver them
until the following morn.

PRESIDING MAGISTRATE:

Not now remembered?

ARMOUR WREN: *(suddenly)*

Ah, now I recall!

PRESIDING MAGISTRATE:

What do you recall, Mister Wren?

ARMOUR WREN:

That is why I instructed James to turn
around. That is why we had a full view
of the whole thing.

CHORUS:

That is why we had a full view of the whole thing.

PRESIDING MAGISTRATE:

And why is that?

ARMOUR WREN:

What I forgot to tell Mister Williamson
was that it would be inconvenient to
deliver them until the morrow.

PRESIDING MAGISTRATE:

For some reason not now remembered?

ARMOUR WREN:

Yes. That is as it happened. What of it, sir?

PRESIDING MAGISTRATE:

Then there is a gap, or gulf, in the factual
evidence, and, consequently, in the truth.

ARMOUR WREN:

Yes, that may well be.

PRESIDING MAGISTRATE:

Mister Wren, you must bear with us in
this examination. It is the business
of this inquest to decide whether Mister
Williamson is alive or dead. If we rule
he is dead, his estate will be distributed
according to the law. I hope you can
appreciate the gravity of the situation.

ARMOUR WREN:

He was a friend and a neighbor. All
I can recall is that just before the . . .

CHORUS:

All I can recall is that just before the . . .

Pause. Something odd happens.

Just before the . . . ah, event . . . he threw
away the stump of a cigar. That is my last
image of him as he strolled leisurely down
the gravel path to the pasture. In broad
daylight, in the middle of an open field.

PRESIDING MAGISTRATE:

In the open and visible?

ARMOUR WREN:

In the open and visible.

PRESIDING MAGISTRATE:

And what happened then, Mister Wren?

ARMOUR WREN:

At that moment one of the coach horses
stumbled and came near falling. It had
no more than fairly recovered itself
when I heard my son James cry out, "Why,
father, what has become of Mister Williamson?"

CHORUS:

Why, father, what has become of Mister Williamson?

PRESIDING MAGISTRATE:

It is not the business of this narrative to answer* that question.

But WREN isn't listening. He goes on, as in a trance.

ARMOUR WREN:

My son's exclamation caused me to look toward the spot where I had seen the . . . where I had seen him only an instant before. But he was not there, nor was he anywhere visible. I cannot say at that moment I was greatly startled, or realized the gravity of the occurrence, though I thought it singular. My son, however, was greatly astonished and kept repeating his question in different forms, even in a greater degree until we arrived at the gate.

End of Second Telling.

INTERLUDE

SCENE [POISON HEMLOCK]

Third Telling. Out of doors. It is morning, not quite ten. The lawn immediately in front of the planter WILLIAMSON's house, six miles from Selma, Alabama. MISTER WILLIAMSON, HIS WIFE, and DAUGHTER are sitting on the veranda. He is leisurely reading the newspaper. The young MOTHER is playing with her CHILD as though she (Mom) were a child, too, which she is.

THE WILLIAMSON GIRL:

I think today is the day we should all stop talking.

MISTER WILLIAMSON:

All stop talking, ha.

MRS. WILLIAMSON:

All stop talking, hurrah.

THE WILLIAMSON GIRL:

I mean I think today would be the
perfect day to drop into the hole
of not talking.

MRS. WILLIAMSON:

Not talking is not a hole, dear.

THE WILLIAMSON GIRL:

Oh, mother, you are a precious fool.

MISTER WILLIAMSON:

You do the stop talking, girl.

MRS. WILLIAMSON:

All stop talking, hurrah!

THE WILLIAMSON GIRL:

All the talking in the world
rounds the world in thirty days.
It never stays. It never stays.

MRS. WILLIAMSON:

Where does it go, then?

THE WILLIAMSON GIRL: *(thinking)*

It goes into a dark hole.
At the bottom of the sea.
Or it turns into a giant. Gruesome.

Bug or beetle. Or a weevil.
A bug of unknowable dimension,
that feeds upon the dead. And the
things of the dead.

MRS. WILLIAMSON:
Sounds a bit gruesome.

MISTER WILLIAMSON: *(aside)*
What's the point of talking that crap.

But both have heard.

MRS. WILLIAMSON: *(starts a little game to clear the air)*
All stop talking, hurrah!

They slap hands.

THE WILLIAMSON GIRL:
Hurrah, hurray! The moon's a hole!

MRS. WILLIAMSON:
Hurrah, hurray! The hole's a who!

THE WILLIAMSON GIRL:
Hurrah, hurray! The who's a what!

MRS. WILLIAMSON :
Hurrah, hurray! The what's a why!

THE WILLIAMSON GIRL:
Hurrah, hurray! The why's a why not!

MRS. WILLIAMSON:

Hurrah, hurray! Why not the moon!

It's so much fun, they repeat it word for word, slap for slap.

THE WILLIAMSON GIRL:

Hurrah, hurray! The moon's a hole!

MRS. WILLIAMSON:

Hurrah, hurray! The hole's a who!

THE WILLIAMSON GIRL:

Hurrah, hurray! The who's a what!

MRS. WILLIAMSON:

Hurrah, hurray! The what's a why!

THE WILLIAMSON GIRL:

Hurrah, hurray! The why's a why not!

MRS. WILLIAMSON:

Hurrah, hurray! Why not the moon!
What color is this giant beetle?
This gruesome bug or weevil?

THE WILLIAMSON GIRL:

Ebony and golden, with glittering
golden eyes. Eyes very penetrant.
Talk turns to gold . . .
Turns to gold when it's told.
Turns to gold when it's told.
Turns to gold when it's told.
Oh,

MRS. WILLIAMSON:

There are more Mysteries in Selma,
in Selma

THE WILLIAMSON GIRL:

in Selma, Alabama.

MRS. WILLIAMSON:

There are more Mysteries in Selma,
Alabama

THE WILLIAMSON GIRL:

Turns to gold when it is told

MRS. WILLIAMSON:

there are more Mysteries in Selma,
Alabama, than . . . than . . .
Than there are bad children in the
Darkman's night school . . .
in the Darkman's night school.
In the Darkman's night school.
Whirling whirling whirling
upon the Darkman's night stool.

BOTH:

Whirling whirling whirling.
Upon the Darkman's night stool.
Upon the Darkman's night stool.

THE WILLIAMSON GIRL:

Oh, mother, you are a precious fool.

MISTER WILLIAMSON:

She is, child, ain't it the truth?

THE WILLIAMSON GIRL:

Father, you are not allowed to
talk. Your talk has been taken
from you because of a bad, bad
thing you did.

MISTER WILLIAMSON:

Bad thing I did, ha!

THE WILLIAMSON GIRL:

A bad thing you did indeed.

MISTER WILLIAMSON:

A thing I did?

THE WILLIAMSON GIRL:

A thing you did. With your head.

MISTER WILLIAMSON:

With my head?

THE WILLIAMSON GIRL:

Precisely, with your head.

MISTER WILLIAMSON:

And you won't tell me what?

THE WILLIAMSON GIRL:

You know very well what.

MISTER WILLIAMSON:

So you won't tell me what.

THE WILLIAMSON GIRL:

You know very well what.

MISTER WILLIAMSON:

So what is it I have done?

Pause.

THE WILLIAMSON GIRL:

You have not talked to the horses.
You have not talked to the horses
about the history of horses,
and about the mysteries of Selma, Alabama.

MRS. WILLIAMSON:

Selma, Alabama. Hurrah, hurray!

MISTER WILLIAMSON:

Ah, the mysteries of Selma.

MRS. WILLIAMSON:

Selma, Alabama. Hurrah, hurray!

THE WILLIAMSON GIRL:

Yes, the mysteries of Selma, Alabama.

MISTER WILLIAMSON:

Ah, the mysteries of Selma, Alabama,
where we reside.

THE WILLIAMSON GIRL:

Which I am dying to learn.
Because I want to know what's right
and what's wrong.

MISTER WILLIAMSON:

What's wrong.

THE WILLIAMSON GIRL:

Because I want to know everything
about everything. Everything that is
and everything that is not. Everything
that appears and goes on for a time
and then goes out. Out and away.

Everything that goes on for a time, and
everything that goes on for a time, and
everything that goes on for a time, and
everything that goes on for a time, and
everything that goes on for a time, and
everything that goes on for a time, and
everything that goes on for a time, and
and disappears.

Like the corn and the cotton and the hay.
Everything that goes away, and everything
that appears to disappear but doesn't really.
Ideas and politics and the history of the
state of Alabama. Oh, mother, oh, father,
what is Selma, Alabama? And why does Selma,
Alabama stay in one place for so long that
we take it for what it appears to be? Why
does Selma, Alabama stay for so long when all
the people, everyone we know, everyone who
lives in Selma, Alabama is bound to go away?
Why, mother, why, father?
What if there is something special,
a something special we don't see?

MRS. WILLIAMSON:

We don't see?

MISTER WILLIAMSON:

That's ridiculous. We see everything.

THE WILLIAMSON GIRL:

Because I want to know what's right and what's wrong.

MISTER WILLIAMSON: *(not hearing)*

What's what?

MRS. WILLIAMSON:

What's wrong. She said, "What's wrong."

THE WILLIAMSON GIRL:

One last thing: I have written a poem about the horses. Only it's not about the horses. It's about something else.

She recites.

Someone or something
carries a candle
in the night, or in
the open and visible,
in broad daylight.

Someone or something:
candle blows out
in the night, or in
the open and visible,
in broad daylight.

Someone or something goes.
Someone or something stays
in the night, or in
the open and visible,
in broad daylight.

MISTER WILLIAMSON:
What's the point of writing down
nonsense like that?

Pause.

THE WILLIAMSON GIRL: *(with mock seriousness)*
Father, you are taking a terrible
risk, you know?

MISTER WILLIAMSON:
Child, what has gotten into you?

MRS. WILLIAMSON:
What has gotten into her indeed? Ha!

THE WILLIAMSON GIRL:
There is a thing that all the talking
in the world cannot stop. And once
it's told it turns to gold . . . as
foretold . . . by a horse.

MISTER WILLIAMSON:
Reminds me. I forgot to tell Andrew
about those horses.

He sets off. End of Third Telling.

SCENE [POISON IVY]

Fourth Telling. Behind the WILLIAMSON *house. A* CHORUS *of slaves. Halfway between them and the scene of the previous Telling and the scene of the impending disappearance is the black boy,* SAM. *He is watching what's happening and then relates it to the members of the* CHORUS.

THE BOY SAM:

Something has happened but I don't know what.

CHORUS:

Don't know what.

THE BOY SAM:

Saw him throw away the stump of his cigar.

CHORUS:

His cigar.

THE BOY SAM:

Saw him stroll real leisurely down that garden path.

CHORUS:

Down that garden path.

THE BOY SAM:

Saw him stroll down that gravel walk.

CHORUS:

Gravel walk.

THE BOY SAM:

Saw him pluck a flower, or did he top it with a stick?

CHORUS:

Topped it with a stick.

THE BOY SAM:

No. As he went he plucked a flower.

CHORUS:

Plucked a flower.

THE BOY SAM:

"Forgot to tell Andrew about those horses," was what he said.

CHORUS:

What he said.

THE BOY SAM:

Funny thing is he ain't the only one.

CHORUS:

Ain't the only one.

THE BOY SAM:

Jim, Mister Wren's son, heard his Dad say something like: "I forgot* to tell Mister Williamson about those horses."

CHORUS:

I forgot to tell Mister Williamson about those horses.

THE BOY SAM:

They're about two hundred yards from the gate now, gate to the open field. Ain't that funny.

Nobody says nothing. SAM is confused by this lack of response.

I said, "Ain't that funny."

The CHORUS *members turn their backs.*

We are building a nation.
We are building a nation.
We are building a nation.
We are building an erasure.

All but SAM *snap their fingers seven times, slow.*

During this, SAM *turns back. Something like a choral gasp of surprise, from the direction of the empty ten-acre field (from the direction of the disappearance).*

We hear a scream from MRS. WILLIAMSON, *who has witnessed the event.*

THE BOY SAM:

Where the devil did he go? Hell, just where the
devil do you think he went?

ONE SLAVE:

Where the devil do you think who went?

THE BOY SAM:

He went.

A SLAVE:

The devil do you think he went.

ANOTHER:

Devil do you think he went.

ANOTHER:

Do you think he went.

ANOTHER:

You think he went.

ANOTHER:

Think he went.

ANOTHER:

He went.

ALL INCLUDING SAM:

Went.

Pause.

CHORUS:

WHERE THE DEVIL DO YOU THINK WHO WENT?

THE BOY SAM:

He went.

A SLAVE:

The* devil do you think he went.

ANOTHER:

Devil* do you think he went.

ANOTHER:

Do* you think he went.

ANOTHER:

You* think he went.

ANOTHER:

Think* he went.

ANOTHER:

He* went.

THE BOY SAM:

Went?

CHORUS:

Went. Went and gone.

A SLAVE:

He's went and gone.

THE BOY SAM:

But where? Sure as hell beats the heck out of me. Where?

He looks back. An OLD WOMAN *comes over to him and puts her arm around him.*

OLD WOMAN:

Sometimes people get the habit of going
back where they first started,
back where the whole thing first got up on
its hind legs and started walking,
walking back to where the thought was
thought that gave us folks the taste of
creation, yeah yeah, the taste of creation.
From the first morning of the world.

CHORUS:

The taste of creation
The taste of creation—yeah, yeah.
The taste of creation.

THE BOY SAM:

And the habit of going back to awful places.
Awful, awful, awful.

OLD WOMAN:

Where the man who's boss-man
sports a cloven hoof. And on
his other a sock of green velvet,
and over that a silver boot.
Where the boss-man is a man like
that. With eyes penetrant.

CHORUS:

With eyes penetrant.

THE BOY SAM:

Oh, oh oh, you mean that.

OLD WOMAN:

We mean that. What you think we mean?

CHORUS:

We mean that.

OLD WOMAN:

Shit, child, is you is,
or is you ain't?

THE BOY SAM:

I think something sheer awful
has happened here.

CHORUS:

Happened here

THE BOY SAM:

I think something that
don't have a name.

CHORUS:

Have a name.

THE BOY SAM:

I think we ought not to misregard whatever it is.

CHORUS:

Whatever it is.

THE BOY SAM:

That's what I think. That's what I think.

CHORUS:

What I think.

THE BOY SAM:

Something with the mask of unavoidability written all over it.

CHORUS:

Written all over it.

THE BOY SAM:

Something sheer awful. That's what I think.

CHORUS:

That's what I think. That's what I think.

OLD WOMAN:

Get along you, you talk too much. No one, not no one's ever going to find out what I think, what I think has happened here. No one. No one. Because I won't disclose it. All I say is: what was, isn't.
What was, isn't. Isn't no more. Because I think I know, and I'm not saying more. Not now anyhow. Because I think I know. Because I think I know. What was, isn't. Isn't no more. Yup. Isn't. Isn't no more.
The mystery of Selma, Alabama is: what was, isn't.

CHORUS:

We are building a nation.
We are building a nation.
We are building a nation.
We are building an erasure.

All but SAM *snap fingers seven times, slow.*

OLD WOMAN:

That's right: what was, isn't. Isn't no more.

She hisses.

VIRGINIA CREEPER:

Where did he go?

THE BOY SAM:

Where did Mister Williamson go?

VIRGINIA CREEPER:

Where did he go?

THE BOY SAM:

Where did Mister Williamson go?

VIRGINIA CREEPER:

Where did he go?

THE BOY SAM:

Where did Mister Williamson go?

End of Fourth Telling.

SCENE [LOCO WEED]

The Fifth Telling. Back at the inquest, just as before. ANDREW, *the Overseer (and* MISTER WILLIAMSON*'s brother) is giving his testimony.*

PRESIDING MAGISTRATE:

And what was your brother's—Mister Williamson's—
advice to you, on the topic of Negro management?

ANDREW:

Similar, very similar to the advice of the late
John C. Calhoun.

CHORUS:

One:

ANDREW:

Never permit any order you give to be disobeyed, or disregarded,
without a strict inquiry into it, & punish the offender if necessary.

CHORUS:

Two:

ANDREW:

Set the first example of strict attention to your duties & you may
with the more justice & propriety inflict punishment upon others
for the neglect of theirs.

CHORUS:

Three:

ANDREW:

Never make an order without punctually attending to it, for if you
make a rule & forget it yourself, with what face can you punish
others for neglecting it also?

CHORUS:

Four:

ANDREW:

If you punish only according to justice & reason, with uniformity, you can never be too severe, & will be the more respected for it, even by those who suffer.

CHORUS:

Five:

ANDREW:

Arrangement & regularity form the great secret of doing things well; you must therefore as far as possible have everything done according to a fixed rule.

Pause.

PRESIDING MAGISTRATE:

A fixed rule?

ANDREW:

A fixed rule.

PRESIDING MAGISTRATE:

What do you suppose he meant by that?

ANDREW:

I suppose he meant a rule that applies to all,
regardless of circumstances. I guess.

Pause.

PRESIDING MAGISTRATE:

And you were in the field beyond?

ANDREW:

I was in the field beyond; yes, I was.
There were perhaps a dozen slaves
working under my. Under my control, that is.

PRESIDING MAGISTRATE:

A dozen slaves you slave?

From the slaves' quarters we hear the

CHORUS:

Slaves you slave.
Slaves you slave.
Slaves you slave.
Slaves you slave.
Slaves you slave.

ANDREW:

A dozen slaves I slave; that is correct.

PRESIDING MAGISTRATE:

And what were their . . . hypothetical attributes,
in the book of heaven, the Book of Higher Things?

ANDREW:

Round, Square, Juniper, Crabgrass, Candlestick, Limbo, Clock,
Bumblebee, Jackass, Crawdad, Nuisance, Puissance, Doorbell, and
Virginia Creeper. That's two more than twelve, but nothing's
perfect, even in the realm of fixed rules.

PRESIDING MAGISTRATE:

How did you arrive at that calculus, by Job?

ANDREW:

By means of the Prince of Gators cigar
that was given to me by my grandfather.

PRESIDING MAGISTRATE:

And what was your grandfather's good name?

ANDREW:

Clock. Grandfather's name was Clock.
His name was Clock. Of the tribe of Clock.
But I fear his true mode of locomotion,
like that of Prince Zandor,* was more
humble: the singleton crutch, or cane.
Of the tribe of Crutch.

WITNESSES:

Prince Zandor! Ah, Prince Zandor!

PRESIDING MAGISTRATE:

Crutch. Are you telling me Crutch?

ANDREW:

Crutch. That is correct. Of the tribe of Crutch.

PRESIDING MAGISTRATE:

And did you overhear any unusual things spoken among them?

ANDREW:

Among who?

PRESIDING MAGISTRATE:

Among the slaves.

ANDREW:

Oh. No, not until later.

PRESIDING MAGISTRATE:

And what did you hear then?

ANDREW:

Only the most . . . the most monstrous
and grotesque fictions, fictions of
course, fictions originating with the
blacks. With the blacks, of course.

PRESIDING MAGISTRATE:

Monstrous and grotesque fictions?

ANDREW:

That's correct, sir—monstrous and grotesque.

PRESIDING MAGISTRATE:

But fictions clearly. You are saying these
things you heard them telling in the slaves'
quarters were fictions clearly? Is that what
you are saying?

Pause.

ANDREW:

That is what I am saying.

PRESIDING MAGISTRATE:

I see.

ANDREW:

You see, Mrs. Williamson had lost her reason,
and the boy, James, had at first declared
he actually witnessed the disappearance;
although later he perhaps wisely, yes,

perhaps wisely changed his tune. And
the Williamson child, a girl, What's-her-name,
has proved a complete ninny and goes about . . .
well, goes about telling how she knew it
was going to happen, yes, was going to happen.
Because of how she had charged her father with,
"You have not talked to the horses.
You have not talked to the horses
about the mysteries of Selma."* I mean it all
quite defies the great secret of doing things
well. By arrangement & regularity.

WITNESSES:
Selma. Selma, Alabama.

PRESIDING MAGISTRATE:
By arrangement & regularity? What do you mean?

ANDREW: *(paying no attention)*
Yes. From Mister Williamson's advice on the
topic of Negro management: arrangement
& regularity form the great secret of doing
things well. Further, the boy, James Wren,
had the good sense to amend his testimony,
I suppose because it was ridiculous
and had the appearance of a fiction.
A monstrous and grotesque fiction.

PRESIDING MAGISTRATE:
His father, Armour Wren, has taken
charge of that, and the black boy, Sam,
being a black boy, is judged incompetent
to give his testimony.

ANDREW:

Yes, yes—that is good.

Pause.

PRESIDING MAGISTRATE:

Good? What the hell is good about it,
Andrew? We have before us the instance
of a fully grown man disappearing
from off of the face of the earth. Disappearing
in full view of family, friends, and the
eye of the Almighty Himself, and you find that
"good"?

ANDREW:

No, sir, that is not what I meant.

PRESIDING MAGISTRATE:

Well, I for one do not find it good. I find
it . . . I find it . . . Damnation, I do not
know how I find it; but I do not find
it good.

ANDREW:

What I meant to suggest was. Oh, hell. None
of the field hands in the field to which Mister
Williamson, my brother, was going had seen
him at all, and the most rigorous search of
the entire plantation and adjoining country failed
to supply a clue.

PRESIDING MAGISTRATE:

And?

ANDREW:

Okay, okay.

PRESIDING MAGISTRATE:

?

ANDREW:

His name was Clock. Of the tribe of Clock.
But I fear his true mode of locomotion,
like that of Prince Zandor, was more
humble: the singleton crutch, or cane.
Of the tribe of Crutch, or Cane.

WITNESSES:

Prince Zandor! Ah, Prince Zandor.

ANDREW:

Yes, Grandfather Clock, wise presence
in the gulf. In the gulf of empty time.
And I know the secret history of horses.
And I know the mysteries of Selma, of
Selma, Alabama: (a) The efficacy of the
Kansas–Nebraska Act, recently passed by
the Congress in Washington, postponing
and prolonging the catastrophe that is
shortly to be upon us; (b) the wit and
glowing wisdom of the late John C. Calhoun,
with his thoughts on the topic of Negro
management; and (c) the arrangement & regularity
of doing things well, which is a great secret . . .
a . . . a great secret to the gulf that has . . .
the gulf that must have yawned up beneath us . . .
that must yawn up beneath us, yawn up
before us, beneath us, all in the open and visible.

So that, so that something or someone,
something heretofore hidden shall be
revealed, and someone or something else
must be nominated an absence and turned
to pure, to purest gold. The gold of reality
translated into that of a fiction. For,
we are building a nation.
We are building a nation.
We are building a nation.
We are building an erasure.
Is you is, or is you ain't?

Long pause. The PRESIDING MAGISTRATE *stands to his full, ghastly height.*

PRESIDING MAGISTRATE:

It is not the purpose of this narrative
to answer that question. This court has
come to a decision. And that decision is
that Williamson is dead, and his estate
shall be distributed according to law.

The Stage World cracks open to reveal the vast openness of Mister Williamson's field. Seen from a steep rake. There is not a tree, nor a shrub, nor an obstruction of any kind visible.

End of Fifth Telling.

SCENE [BLACK NIGHTSHADE]

The Sixth Telling. The open field of MISTER WILLIAMSON *on a morning in July 1854, six miles from Selma, Alabama. Light pours level across the newly plowed land. We see* WILLIAMSON *enter from downstage left and close the gate of the field. He walks slowly across the field and plucks a flower as he goes, heading diagonally to upstage right.*

WILLIAMSON:

What is the point of talking crap like that?
I had no reason to think she had at that time lost her mind
Light poured level across the open field
I threw away the stump of my cigar and opened the gate
Something about those horses I had forgotten to remember to tell . . .
To tell someone . . .

To tell someone something . . .
Light, light poured level across the open field as I entered and closed the gate behind me.
I walked slowly across the field and plucked a flower, or did I top it with a stick
I had no reason to think she had at that time lost her mind
He is gone, she said, he's gone
Music and shadow passed over me and I was gone
She was right, I was gone

He disappears.

THE WILLIAMSON GIRL:

What* is the point of talking crap like that, Round?
What is the point of talking crap like that, Square?
What is the point of talking crap like that, Juniper?
What is the point of talking crap like that, Crabgrass?
What is the point of talking crap like that, Candlestick?
What is the point of talking crap like that, Limbo?
What is the point of talking crap like that, Clock?
What is the point of talking crap like that, Bumblebee?
What is the point of talking crap like that, Jackass?
What is the point of talking crap like that, Crawdad?
What is the point of talking crap like that, Nuisance?
What is the point of talking crap like that, Puissance?

What is the point of talking crap like that, Doorbell?
What is the point of talking crap like that, Virginia Creeper?
What is the point of talking crap like that, Jim?
What is the point of talking crap like that, Sam?
What is the point of talking crap like that, What's-her-name?

THE BOY SAM:
Something has happened, but I don't know
what.* What? Saw him throw away the
stump of his cigar. Saw him stroll real
leisurely down that garden path. Saw
him stroll down that gravel walk. Saw
him pluck a flower as he went. Or did he
top it with a stick? Where the devil do
you think he went? But where? Sometimes
people get the habit of going back where
the whole thing started. Back where
what is, is not. Where what is, is not.
Where what is, is not. Is not no more.
I think something sheer awful
has happened, something that
don't have a name. That's what I think.
That's what I think.

VIRGINIA CREEPER: *(?)*
Why . . .
Whatever do you think has happened to Mister Williamson?

Repeat over and over till the Black Folk follow. They sing a wordless prayer of thanks.

End of Sixth Telling.

SCENE [FOXGLOVE]

The Seventh Telling. MRS. WILLIAMSON *is up on the roof of the house, alone. All freeze below.*

MRS. WILLIAMSON:

I had no reason to think I had
at the time lost my mind. It
was only that I have never
seen nor heard of Mister
Williamson since that moment.
I do believe I said something
like, "He is gone! He is gone! Oh God,
he is gone! He is gone! Oh God,
what an awful thing!" and
many other such exclamations,
which I do not distinctly
recollect. I got from them
the impression that they were
related to something more than
the mere disappearance of my husband.

He is gone. He is gone. Oh, God.
Something more than a mere disappearance
even if, as if that had occurred before
my very eyes. Which it did. My manner
was wild, but not more so, I think, than
was natural under the circumstances, yes,
than was indeed natural under the . . . the
circumstances. I have no reason to
think I had at the time lost my mind.
Lost her reason, they said.
And was, like the servants, unable
to testify. "He is gone! He is gone!

Oh, God, what an awful thing."
I have never seen nor heard of Mister
Williamson. Nor of Mrs. Williamson since.
Something more than a mere disappearance.
More than a mere disappearance.
Than a mere disappearance.
A mere disappearance.

THE WILLIAMSON GIRL: *(half hidden, whispering)*
Someone or something knows
something someone or something
will not tell.

No one knows what telling
is the one someone or (something)
will not tell.

THE BOY SAM:
He must've been called away
on urgent business.

THE WILLIAMSON GIRL:
I hope people will not think
I wished for it to happen, Sam.
I did not wish for it to happen.
It happened all by itself, I swear.

MRS. WILLIAMSON:
Who swears? Who swears?

THE BOY SAM:
All James said was, "Why, father, what has
become of Mister Williamson?"

THE WILLIAMSON GIRL:

Why is Mother up there on the roof? Oh,
Sam, do you think I did something
in my head? Do you think it's because
I said, "Father.

CHORUS:

You have not talked to the horses.
You have not talked to the horses
about the history of horses,
and the mysteries of Selma."

Pause.

ONE SLAVE:

Selma, Alabama.

VIRGINIA CREEPER:

Ah, the Mysteries of Selma, ah!

ANOTHER SLAVE:

Selma, Alabama.

THE WILLIAMSON GIRL:

All about the mysteries of Selma, Selma,
Alabama, which I was dying to learn.

THE BOY SAM:

Oh, I don't know. I don't know
what I should say? Should I say
I saw a disappearance. How can you
say that you saw a disappearance?

THE WILLIAMSON GIRL:

Say what you saw.

MRS. WILLIAMSON:

Say what you saw, boy. You saw
something more than a mere disappearance.
You saw the same thing I saw, didn't you?

THE BOY SAM:

No, Mrs. Williamson, no, no, no.
I saw your husband, Mister Williamson,
just as you did.

MRS. WILLIAMSON:

That's what I am saying.
That's what I am saying.
That's why I am staying up here
on the roof. I am staying up here
till they tell me this is a fiction,
and I am not who I am, boy.

THE WILLIAMSON GIRL, SAM, AND VIRGINIA CREEPER:

Not who I am, boy.
Not who I am, boy.
Not who I am, boy.

All THREE *snap their fingers seven times, slow.*

THE WILLIAMSON GIRL:

I wasn't looking, Sam. James,
my face was following the line of a crow
as it followed the line of the sky, as it
followed the line of the day, as it followed
the line of someone or something:

Someone or something who knows
something someone or something

will not tell.
No one knows what telling
is the one that someone (or something)
will not tell.

CHORUS:
Who knows?

THE BOY SAM:
Saw him throw away the stump of his cigar.

VIRGINIA CREEPER:
Throw away the stump of a cigar.
Or topped that flower with a stick.

THE BOY SAM:
How did you know?

VIRGINIA CREEPER:
That's what you said.

THE BOY SAM:
No. I said, "No."
He plucked a flower instead.

ANOTHER:
Plucked a flower: ain't that sweet.

CHORUS:
Ain't that sweet.

THE BOY SAM:
Now I don't know which.

ANOTHER:

Don't know which.

CHORUS:

He don't know which.

ANOTHER:

"Forgot to tell Andrew about those horses,"
was what he said.

THE BOY SAM:

How did you know?

CHORUS:

We all know.

ANOTHER:

And Mister Wren told the coachman, "Turn
round. I forgot to tell Mister Williamson
about those horses."

THE BOY SAM:

How did you know?

CHORUS:

We all know.

ANOTHER:

I know.

VIRGINIA CREEPER:

I know.

CHORUS:

We all know.

THE BOY SAM:

But how? How?

A silence, immense and tangible.

VIRGINIA CREEPER:

Like you say.

CHORUS:

We all know.

ANOTHER:

We saw Mister Williamson walking real leisurely across the open field.

CHORUS:

We all know.

ANOTHER:

And at that moment one of our coach horses stumbled, and came near falling.

CHORUS:

We all know.

VIRGINIA CREEPER:

Came near falling. We all know.

CHORUS:

We all know.

The members of the CHORUS *snap their fingers seven times, slow.*

THE BOY SAM:

It had no more recovered itself
when James cried out,

THE WILLIAMSON GIRL, SAM, AND VIRGINIA CREEPER:

Why, father, what has become of Mister
Williamson?

CHORUS:

We all know.

MRS. WILLIAMSON:

That's what I* am saying.
That's what I am saying.
That's why I am staying up here
on the roof. I am staying here
till they tell me this is a fiction
and I am not who I am, girl.

VIRGINIA CREEPER AND SAM:

Why, father,* what has become of Mister Williamson?
What has become of Mister Williamson?

THE WILLIAMSON GIRL:

Why, father, what has become of Mister Williamson?
Why, father, what has become of Mister Williamson?
Why, father, what has become of Mister Williamson?

THE WILLIAMSON GIRL:

Someone or something
carries a candle
in the night, or in

the open and visible,
in broad daylight.

Someone or something:
candle blows out
in the night, or in
the open and visible,
in broad daylight.

Someone or something goes.
Someone or something stays
in the night, or in
the open and visible,
in broad daylight.

Someone or something
without its ghost

in the night, or in
the open and visible,
in broad daylight.

End of Seventh Telling.

End of play.

Bitter Bierce; or,
The Friction We Call Grief

Bitter Bierce (based on the life and writing of Ambrose Bierce) premiered at P.S. 122 in 2003 under the author's direction.

SETTING

A large open room, things arranged as for a public lecture.

We see AMBROSE BIERCE*—a tall, elegant, and very capable looking man—alone, standing behind a wooden table; there is something a little apparitional about his good looks (and why does not the apparition of a suit of clothes sometimes walk abroad without a ghost in it?); on the table is a cabbage—an elegant, very capable looking and quite green—cabbage.*

Reality, noun.
The dream of a mad philosopher.
That which remains in the cupel if one
should assay a phantom. The nucleus of a
vacuum.

Realism, noun.
The art of depicting nature as it is seen by
toads.

—

Disobedience, noun.
The silver lining in the cloud of servitude.

Zigzag, verb transitive.
To move forward uncertainly, from side
to side, as one carrying the white man's
burden.

—

My country 'tis of thee,
sweet land of felony,
 of thee I sing;
land where my fathers fried
young witches and applied
whips to the Quaker's hide,
 and made him spring.

They call me "Bitter Bierce."

"A purveyor of morbidities."

"Sado-masochistic," says the good doctor Isaac Goldberg.

"Bierce is as interesting as a kangaroo," in the opinion of J. S. Cowley-Brown, whoever he was.

My great-great-great-great-grandfather, Austin Bearse, sailed on the good ship *Confidence* in 1638 from Southhampton and landed at Barnstable on Cape Cod. There are still Bearses on Cape Cod no doubt, stirring up trouble.

Troubling the pious with rational language.

Language, noun.
The music with which we charm the serpents guarding another's treasure.

Rational, adjective.
Devoid of all delusions save those of observation, experience, and reflection.

Piety, noun.
Reverence for the supreme being, based on his supposed resemblance to man.

—

From a flyleaf of the family bible printed in 1699: Marquis, said Louis XIV to Marquis de Bearse, you make puns on all subjects. Make one on me. Sire, replied the courteous Marquis, you are no *subject.*

—

My uncle, General Lucius Verus Bierce, organized "The Grand Eagles," a secret society of some three hundred crested idiots to invade Canada and free her from the despotism of Sir John Coburn. The British struck first and virtually annihilated the force. Uncle retreated to Swan Lake to reorganize. He told the remnant, Canadian liberty depends on you.

On returning to Ohio, Uncle Lucius Verus was called before the United States Court at Columbus to answer for his violation of the Neutrality Law of 1818.

Meanwhile, my own family migrated to Horse Cave, Ohio, where I was born on the 24th of June, 1842. When I was still quite young, we moved to Indiana, an even more drab and featureless place. Flat and Dull and, in the summers, unbearably warm.

My father, Marcus Aurelius Bierce, was of altogether a more somber (not to mention *mediocre*) disposition. And both my parents were afflicted by the madness of religion; Religion, that daughter of Hope and Fear, who is in the habit of explaining to Ignorance the nature of the Unknowable.

My siblings' names all begin with a capital *A:* Abigail Bell, Amelia Josephine, Ann Maria, Addison Byron, Aurelius, Almeda Sophia, Albert Sherwood, Augustus, and yours truly, Ambrose Gwinett.

A dream.
I am traveling in darkness through a fire-swept region. Pools of water glimmer in shallow depressions, as if the fire had been followed by rain. A crimson light burns in the West. Which reminds me in later years of a painting by Doré. Battlements loom up before me. Wandering around in the monstrous building I come into a large room full of the same gleaming phantasmagorical light. Upon a bed a figure lies—the features are my own.

—

Early one morning in 1872, I murdered my father—an act that made a deep impression on me at the time. This was before my marriage when I was living with my parents in Wisconsin. My father and I were in the library of our home, dividing the proceeds of a burglary that we had committed that night. These consisted of household goods mostly, and the task of equitable division was difficult. We got on very well with the napkins, towels, and such things, and the silverware was parted pretty nearly equally, but you can see for yourself that when you try to divide a single music box by two without a remainder you will have trouble. It was that music box which brought disaster and disgrace upon our family. If we had left it, my poor father might now be alive.

It was the most exquisite and beautiful piece of workmanship—inlaid with costly woods and carven very curiously. It would not only play a great variety of tunes but would whistle like a quail, bark like a dog, crow every morning at daylight whether it was wound up or not, and break the ten commandments. It was this last-mentioned accomplishment that won my father's heart and caused him to commit the only dishon orable act of his life.

Though possibly he would have committed more if he had been spared. He tried to conceal that music box from me and declared upon his honor that he had not taken it, though I knew very well that, so far as he was concerned, the burglary had been undertaken chiefly for the purpose of obtaining it.

My father had the music box hidden under his cloak; we had worn cloaks by way of disguise. He had solemnly assured me, but I knew that he had. . . .

A small axe, which we had used to break into the unlucky house, lay between us on the table; I picked it up. The old man seeing that further concealment was useless took the box from under his cloak and set it on the table. Cut it in two if you prefer that, he said; I tried to save it from destruction.

He was a passionate lover of music and could himself play the concertina with expression and feeling.

I said: I do not question the purity of your motive: it would be presumptuous in me to sit in judgment on my father. But business is business, and with this axe I am going to effect a dissolution of our partnership unless you will consent in all future burglaries to wear a bell punch.

No, he said, after some reflection, no, I could not do that; people would say that you distrusted me.

I could not help admiring his spirit and sensitiveness; for a moment I was proud of him and disposed to overlook his fault, but a glance at the richly jeweled music box decided me; and as I said, I removed the old man from this vale of tears.

That afternoon I went to the chief of police, told him what I had done, and asked his advice. It would be very painful to me if the facts became publicly known. My conduct would be generally condemned; the newspapers would bring it up against me if ever I should run for office. The chief saw the force of these considerations; he himself was an assassin of wide experience.

—

He holds up the cabbage.

Cabbage, noun.
A familiar kitchen vegetable about as large and wise as a human head.

Saint, noun.
A dead sinner revised and edited.

My early schooling was very rudimentary. My uncle Lucius Verus, however, arranged for my attendance at the Kentucky Military Institute. In addition to the principles of the military, I studied draftsmanship and mapmaking—those who have had occasion to examine them have been invariably amazed by the high quality of the maps and other cartoons that I prepared during the Civil War. But I was only there for a year. The place burned down, and soon after came the war.

I returned home and enlisted on April 19th, 1861, and was assigned to the 9th Indiana Infantry. This was four days after President Lincoln announced the enforcement of the laws of Union, and requested a volunteer force of seventy-five thousand for that purpose.

The 9th Indiana was sent to Virginia, to the Cheat River Valley. That region has ever since been (for me) a kind of dreamland, for the first engagements of the war were sham battles, opéra bouffe affairs. Many of us Indiana and Ohio boys had never seen a mountain before, and here were we, perched on the crest of the Alleghanies, watching the faint graying of the blue above the main range—smoke of the enemy camp.

With what pure delight we inhaled its fragrances of spruce and pine! How we stared with something like awe at its clumps of laurel, whose foliage had been accounted excellent for the heads of illustrious Romans. We carved its roots into finger rings and pipes. We gathered spruce gum and sent it to our sweethearts in letters. Then there is the matter of what I saw, only a few months later, at Shiloh.

The 9th Indiana had been held in reserve, and so we were absent when Johnston's Confederates surprised Grant's army very early Sunday morning April 9th, 1862, and drove them back to the banks of the Tennessee. But within minutes of the alarum, we were running, along with the rest of General Buell's army, the whole eight miles to Pittsburgh Landing.

We passed the last vestiges of forest and came to the place where the battle had raged. Pools of water filled the depressions of earth, discs of rainwater tinged with blood. The force of the fighting was shown by the leafless trees, the blackened stumps. Knapsacks were strewn about and the debris of battle littered the field. Bodies of dead horses were pitched against trees and cannon caissons; ammunition wagons were capsized; broken timbers dotted the ground as though thrown about by the wind of a hurricane.

There were men enough, all dead apparently; except one who lay near where I halted my platoon—a Federal sergeant, variously hurt, who had been a fine giant in his time. He lay face upward, taking in his breath in convulsive, rattling snorts, and blowing it out in sputters of froth that crawled creamily down his cheek. A bullet had clipped a groove in his skull, above the temple; from this the brain protruded in bosses, dropping off in flakes and strings.

Later, I obtained leave to visit a ravine where a company of Illinois men had been surrounded and, refusing to surrender, had been shot to the man. The woods had caught fire, and both living and dead had been cremated. Some lay in attitudes denoting sudden death by bullet, but by far greater number in postures of agony that told of tormenting flame. Some were swollen to double girth; others shriveled to manikins. Faces were bloated and black or yellow and shrunken. The contraction of muscles that had given claws for hands had cursed each countenance with a hideous grin. Faugh!

Those fifteen hours have a grip on my soul to this day. The dark roiling forces of an unseen fate rolled across the plateau; I know what I saw: heroism go down to unutterable defeat before the ruthless idiocy of chance. For I believe that in the word *chance* we have the human name of a malign and soulless intelligence bestirring himself in earthly affairs with the brute unrest of Enceladus underneath his mountain.

History, noun.
An account, mostly false, of events, mostly unimportant, which are brought about by rulers, mostly knaves, and soldiers, mostly fools.

Historian, noun.
A broad-gauge gossip.

—

Ghost, noun.
The outward and visible sign of an inward fear.

There is one insuperable obstacle to belief in ghosts. A ghost never comes naked: he appears either in a winding sheet or "in his habit as he died." To believe in him, then, is to believe that not only have the dead the power to make themselves visible after there is nothing left of them, but that the same power inheres in textile fabrics.

Supposing the products of the loom to have this ability, what object would they have in exercising it? And why does not the apparition of a suit of clothes sometimes walk about without a ghost in it?

These be riddles of significance. They reach way down and get a convulsive grasp on the very taproot of this flourishing faith.

Grave, noun.
A place where the dead are laid to await the coming of the medical student.

Gravitation, noun.
The tendency of all bodies to approach one another with a strength proportioned to the quantity of matter they contain—the quantity of matter they contain being ascertained by the strength of their tendency to approach one another. This is a lovely and edifying

illustration of how science, having made A the proof of B, makes B the proof of A.

Geology, noun.
The geological formations of the globe are catalogued thus: The Primary, or lower one, consists of rocks, bones of mired mules, gas pipes, miners' tools, antique statues minus the nose, Spanish doubloons, and ancestors. The Secondary is largely made up of red worms and moles. The Tertiary comprises railway tracks, patent pavements, grass, snakes, moldy boots, beer bottles, tomato cans, intoxicated citizens, garbage, Anarchists, snap-dogs, and fools.

And Fools.

And fools. Chickamauga.

We'll skip Chickamauga for now.

Missionary Ridge. And on and on.

First a year.

—

Then another.

While serving in the 9th Indiana, I moved with the Army of the Cumberland as it continued south in its march of destruction. The enemy crossed our path at Kennesaw Mountain.

On the 23rd day of June, 1864, General Hazen wrote to his superior: I was ordered to advance my skirmish line, which I attempted to do by sending my topographical engineer, Lieutenant Bierce, to direct it and cause it to be done. While engaged in this duty, Lieutenant Bierce was shot in the head by a musket ball, which caused a very dangerous and complicated wound, the ball remaining within the head from which it was removed sometime afterward.

Carried back to Hospital No. 1 at Chattanooga. We were all loaded on flatcars covered with a tarp and left alone for hours with only the moon to commiserate with our agonies.

Went home to Elkhart, Indiana. I saw that it was still flat and dull, and was still unbearably warm in the summer.

The farms were rundown; the towns were deserted; my head was broken like a walnut.

—

I was finally mustered out of the army at Huntsville, Alabama, in January 1865. I was brevetted major in August by President Andrew Johnson, for "distinguished service during the war." The brevet was of course purely honorary.

It had been my good fortune to command a company of soldiers—real soldiers. Not professional lifelong fighters, the products of European militarism—just plain, ordinary American, volunteer soldiers, who loved their country and fought for it with never a thought of grabbing it for themselves; that is a trick that the survivors were taught by gentlemen desiring their votes.

Eventually moved west, west to San Francisco. Worked briefly at the U.S. Mint. Stayed in various rooming houses off Market Street, near the Mercantile Library. Read books and began to write for publications like the *News-Letter,* whose managing editor was James Watkins. He taught me how to read. I discovered Swift and Voltaire. Shakespeare and Sir Thomas Browne. He taught me how to write.

In one letter to me he mentioned La Rochefoucauld, Murcer, and Balzac and explained: "Your method of language is that of these Frenchmen; your method of thought, meanwhile, is essentially different from theirs; it is the real English (or American) thought and you give us the net result of its processes phrased with the Frenchman's wit and point and epigram."

I came to the conclusion that we think in words. We cannot think without them. Shallowness or obscurity of language means shallowness or obscurity of thought.

To feel rightly one must think and know rightly. And so I took over the "Town Crier" column for the *News-Letter* and became a professional writer.

All in all this was the San Francisco of the Ancient & Honorable Order of the *E. Clampus Vitus,* whose motto is *Credo Quia Absurdum* (I believe because it *is* absurd), and whose members congregate at the Hall of Comparative Ovations; there are an endless array of strange creatures and crested idiots here, like The Great Unknown, Old Rosey, the Money King, and all manner of egregious scalawags, Elks, and Masons; this is the San Francisco of Emperor Norton the First, at whose death the *Bulletin* proclaimed, "The Emperor killed nobody, robbed nobody and deprived nobody of his country, which is more than can be said for most fellows in his trade."

And then there are the Holy Rollers.

Indeed, what a procession of holy idiots we have had in San Francisco—hot gospelers and devil pelters of all degree! Thick-necked Moody with Sankey of the nasal name; Hallenbeck, Earle, Knops, and all their he-harlotry of horribles. And now this grease-eating and salt-crusted Harrison from the pork regions of the Northeast, thinking holy hog and hominy and talking his teeth loose for the dissuasion of sinners from their natural diet of sin without which they would be sick! Can we do nothing to rid us of the periodical incursions of these scale-bugs—these leaf worms—these phylloxera of the moral vineyard? May the devil smite them with a tempest of sulfuric acid from his Babcock extinguisher.

Pray, verb transitive.
To ask that the laws of the universe be annulled on behalf of a single petitioner confessedly unworthy.

Cabbage, I repeat: noun.
A familiar kitchen vegetable about as large and wise as a human head.

—

As for the likes of the Reverend Doughbrane, Reverend Twackbible Shrike,
and Brother Mortificationoftheflesh
J. Mucker . . .

No sane man of intelligence will plead for religion on the ground that it is better than nothing. It is not better than nothing if it is not true. Truth is better than anything, or all things; the next best thing to truth is absence of error. For no one but Jesus Christ ever loved mankind, and look where it got him.

And look where it got him.

—

The seabird speeding from the realm of night
Dashed to death against the beacon light.
Learn from its evil fate, ambitious soul,
The ministry of light is guide, not goal.

As for politics.

Politician, noun.
An eel in the fundamental mud upon which the superstructure of organized society is reared.

Senate, noun.
A body of elderly gentlemen charged with high duties and misdemeanors.

As for California politics.
If nonsense were black, Sacramento would need gas lamps on Monday morning. So scurvy a crew I do not remember outside the carcass of a dead horse. The frosty truth of the situation is that we are a state and a nation of benighted and boasting hypocrites, in whom the moral sense is as dead as Queen Anne at her deadest; that we are floundering and foundering in a sea of public and private corruption as offensive as that upon which the Ancient Mariner saw the shiny things that "did crawl with legs"; that we are a laughingstock to Europe and a menace to civilization.

I ask you, is it blasphemous to hold the mirror up to the blasphemer? Futile, futile, futile.

As for San Francisco.
There is so much hypocrisy among the god's elect in this city. There is even a political party now whose motto is, simply, the Chinese must go.

The dead body of a Chinese woman was found last Tuesday morning lying across the sidewalk in a very uncomfortable position. The cause of her death could not be ascertained, but as her head was caved in, it is thought by some physicians that she died of galloping Christianity of the malignant California type.

Only last Monday two little Christians (with a big *C*) were up before his Honor (with a big *H*) for pelting a Chinaman with rocks. On account of their youth, good character, color, nationality, religion, and the politics of their fathers, they were let off with a reprimand.

This is the kind of thing one finds in the majority of our newspapers.

To feel rightly one must think and know rightly.

Newspapers! They are faithful to nothing but the follies and vices of our system, while strenuously opposing every intelligent attempt at the elimination of these. Newspapers fetter the feet of wisdom and stiffen the prejudices of the ignorant.

They are sycophants to the mob, tyrants to the individual.

And tyrants to the individual.

—

Only last Tuesday a Chinaman passing guilelessly along Dupont Street was assailed with a tempest of bricks and stones from the steps of the First Congregational Church. At the completion of this devotional exercise the Sunday scholars retired within the hallowed portals of the sanctuary, to hear about Christ Jesus, and him crucified.

O, Lord, who for the purposes of this supplication we assume to have created the heavens and earth before man created thee; and who, let us say, art from everlasting to everlasting; we beseech thee to turn thy attention this way and behold a set of the most abandoned scalawags Thou has ever had the pleasure of setting eyes on. But in consideration of the fact that thou sentest thy only-begotten Son among us, and afforded us the felicity of murdering him, we would respectfully suggest the propriety of taking into heaven such of us as pay our church dues, giving us an eternity of exalted laziness and absolutely inconceivable fun. We ask this in the name of thy Son, whom we strung up as before stated. Amen.

—

The ministry of light is guide not goal.

He coughs: the old asthma.

—

In London, they call the air "smog," after the combination of smoke and fog; given the blend of dust and fog in San Francisco, I propose we call it "dog."

Alone, adjective.
Bad company.

Defenseless, adjective.
Unable to attack.

Self-evident, adjective.
Evident to one's self and to nobody else.

—

Meekness, noun.
Uncommon patience in planning a revenge
that is worthwhile.
M is for Moses
who slew the Egyptian.
As sweet as a rose is
the meekness of Moses.
No monument shows his
postmortem inscription.
But M is for Moses
who slew the Egyptian.

Medicine, noun.
A stone flung down the Bowery
to kill a dog in Broadway.

M is for Mollie.

—

The facts about how and when I met Mollie Day are lost. There are no letters, no love poems, no story of the meeting or the courting. The earliest hint of acquaintance appears in the Crier's column of February 5, 1870: "Mollie, tell your mother not to relax her efforts to keep you from writing us. The chances are the old lady is right."

Around this time I wrote and published my first story, "The Haunted Valley,"
about a gnarled, vicious, and xenophobic miner who had murdered his Chinese assistant (perhaps a transvestite) in a jealous rage after suspecting him or her of developing a passion for another miner.

—

Spent a lot of time picnicking, boating, and walking in the hills of San Raphael. No doubt the Days disapproved of me, as well they should. The *News-Letter* received a series of taunting resolutions from such female suffragers as Eliza Straitlace, Jane Squinteye, and Medora Sawnose to the following effect:

THAT whereas the implacable reviler of women and the marriage relation . . .

be caught in the pit which he himself digged;

THAT the sympathies of this society and of the world are bestowed upon the heroic woman who has offered herself a victim upon the altar of that dreadful being's desire to be received into good society;

THAT for her unsuspected, unheralded, and unsurpassed disinterestedness she ought to be relieved at an early date from the purgatory of such a marital existence, into the haven of widowhood;

THAT he is no better than he should be;

THAT it serves him right.

Mollie's father was an old New York Dutchman by the name of Holland Hines Day; he'd struck it rich with the Tintic Mine near Salt Lake City; he did not oppose the match; in fact, Mr. Day promised the newlyweds an all-expense-paid trip to London. A promise that was duly executed.

Love, noun.
A temporary insanity curable by marriage.

—

In this city, married, December 25th, 1871, by Horatio Stebbins, Ambrose G. Bierce and Mary E. Day.

They stood before the altar and supplied
The fire themselves in which their fat was fried.
In vain the sacrifice! No god will claim
An offering burnt with an unholy flame.

Bride, noun.
A woman with a fine prospect of happiness behind her.

—

My farewell to the *News-Letter* appeared on March 9th, 1872:
With this number of the *News-Letter* the present writer's connection with it ceases for at least a brief season. That he has always been entertaining he does not claim, that he has been uniformly good natured is no further true than that he has refrained from actually killing anybody; that he has been "genial" is not true at all. It must be pretty evident that in penning some six or eight thousand paragraphs he must have told a great number of harmless lies and perpetrated divers cruel slanders. For the former he is responsible to his maker, and shall offer no apology; for the latter no apologies would avail, even if he were in the humor of making them—which he is not.

Be as decent as you can. Don't believe without evidence. Treat divine things with respect—don't have anything to do with them. Do not trust humanity without collateral security; it will play you some scurvy trick. Remember that it hurts no one to be treated as an enemy entitled to respect until he shall prove himself a friend worthy of affection. Cultivate a taste for distasteful truths. And, finally, most important of all, endeavor to see things as they are, not as they ought to be.

—

I liked London. I liked England, and acquired some of the mannerisms of that proud race. Wrote under the pseudonym of "Dod Grile." Somehow it didn't catch on the way "Mark Twain" did. My two sons, Leigh and Day, were born there. Did tolerably well, but never made enough money. The weather was hell on my asthma, which became worse.

Met a lot of the best English writers: Tom Hood, the editor of *Fun*; and John Cambden Hotten, publisher of both Twain and Artemus Ward. It was Hotten who suggested I publish my first two books: *Nuggets and Dust* and *Cobwebs from an Empty Skull. The Fiend's Delight* followed in 1874. Had a great deal to worry about: more work than I could do; Mollie having two babies and a nursemaid to look after. Yes, up to my ears in work, grinding stuff for five publications: one semiweekly, two weeklies, one monthly, and one occasional—a pizen thing of which I wrote every line.

In the spring of 1875 my wife decided to return to America; when she got there I got word she was once more pregnant. If this had not been the case, I probably should have stayed, but no.

—

When John Hotten died, shortly before my own departure, a group of his friends gathered to see who could come up with the best epitaph:

Any Guess?

Hotten. Rotten. Forgotten.

—

Actually, adverb.
Perhaps; possibly.

Really, adverb.
Apparently.

White, adjective.
Black.

Returned home in the fall of 1875 and spent most of the winter with wife and children in San Francisco, where we lived at the home of Mr. and Mrs. Day on Vallejo Street.

Took a brief holiday in December to Calistoga Hot Springs, and spent time in Napa.

Began to think about my experiences. In the war. In the woods. In England I had almost forgotten about the strangeness of the woods.

—

He to whom the portentous conspiracy of night and silence and solitude in the heart of a great forest is not an unknown experience needs not to be told what another world it all is. How even the most commonplace and familiar objects take on another character. . . .

There are sounds without a name, forms without substance, translation in space of objects that have not been seen to move, movements wherein nothing is observed to change its place. Ah, children of the sunlight and the gaslight, how little you know of the world in which you live.

Surrounded at a little distance by armed and watchful friends, Byring felt utterly alone. Yielding himself to the solemn and mysterious spirit of the time and place, he had forgotten the nature of his connection with the visible and audible aspects and phases of the night. The forest was boundless; men and the habitations of men did not exist. The universe was one primeval mystery of darkness without form and void, himself the sole, dumb questioner of its eternal secret. Absorbed in thoughts born of this mood, he suffered the time to slip away unnoted. Meantime the infrequent patches of white light lying amongst the tree trunks had undergone changes of size, form, and place. In one of them nearby, just at the roadside, his eye fell upon an object that he had not previously observed. It was almost before his face as he sat; he could have sworn that it had not before been there. It was partly covered in shadow, but he could see that it was a human figure. Instinctively he adjusted the clasp of his sword-belt and laid hold of his pistol—again he was in a world of war, by occupation an assassin.

The figure did not move. Rising, pistol in hand, he approached. The figure lay upon its back, the upper part in shadow, but standing above it and looking down upon the face, he saw that it was a dead body. He shuddered and turned from it with a feeling of sickness and disgust, resumed his seat upon the log, and forgetting military prudence struck a match and lit a cigar. In the sudden blackness that followed the extinction of the flame he felt a sense of relief; he could no longer see the object of his aversion. Nevertheless, he kept his eyes set in that direction until it appeared again with growing distinctness. It seemed to have moved a trifle nearer.

Damn that thing, he muttered. What does it want?

Early the next morning a fatigue party, commanded by a captain and accompanied by a surgeon, searched the ground for dead and wounded. At the fork of the road, a little to one side, they found two bodies lying close together—that of a Federal officer and that of a Confederate private. The officer had died of a sword thrust through the heart, but not apparently until he had inflicted upon his enemy no fewer than five dreadful wounds. The dead officer lay on his face in a pool of blood, the weapon still in his breast. They turned him on his back, and the surgeon removed it. Gad, said the captain, it is Byring, adding with a glance at the other, they had a tough tussle.

The surgeon examined the sword. It was that of a line officer of the Federal infantry—exactly like the one worn by the captain. It was, in fact, Byring's own. The only other weapon found was an undischarged revolver in the dead officer's belt.

The surgeon looked at the captain. The captain looked at the surgeon.

—

A man stood upon a railroad bridge at Owl Creek, in northern Alabama, looking down into the swift water twenty feet below. The man's hands were tied behind his back, the wrists bound with a cord. A rope loosely encircled his neck. It was attached to a stout cross-timber above his head, and the slack fell to the level of his knees.

—

Worm's meat, noun.
The finished product of which we are the raw material.

Rear, noun.
In military parlance, that part of the army that is closest to Congress.

Youth, noun.
The period of possibility, when Archimedes finds a fulcrum, Cassandra has a following, and seven cities compete for the honor of endowing a living Homer.

Youth is the true Saturnian reign, the Golden Age on earth again, when figs are grown on thistles, and pigs betailed with whistles, wearing silver bristles, live ever in clover, and cows fly overhead, delivering milk at every door, and justice never is heard to snore, and every assassin is made a ghost, and howling, is cast into Baltimore.

Un-American, adjective.
Wicked, intolerable, heathenish.

—

(This definition, you will please note, has become general.)

Zeus, noun.
The chief of the Grecian gods, adored by the Romans as Jupiter, and by the modern Americans as God, Gold, Mob, and Dog.

W (double *U*) has, of all the letters in our alphabet, the only cumbrous name, the names of the others being monosyllabic. There can be no doubt whatever that by simplifying the name of *W* our civilization could be, if not promoted, at least, better endured.

Calling it "wow" for example.

—

The Moral Principle and the Material Interest.

A Moral Principle met a Material Interest on a bridge wide enough for but one.

Down you base thing, thundered the Moral Principle, let me pass over you.

The Material Interest merely looked into the other's eyes without saying anything.

Ah, said the Moral Principle hesitatingly, let us draw lots to see which shall retire till the other has crossed.

The Material Interest maintained an unbroken silence and an unwavering stare.

In order to avoid a conflict, the Moral Principle resumed somewhat uneasily, I shall myself lie down and let you walk over me.

Then the Material Interest found a tongue, and by a strange coincidence it was its own tongue.

I don't think you are very good walking,
it said, I am a little particular about what I have
underfoot. Suppose you get off into the water.
It occurred that way.

In the winter of 1889, I made an accidental
discovery of some love letters written to
Mollie by a certain Danish gentleman who
had been summering in St Helena. I told
her, I don't take part in competitions—even
in love.

There was a scene.
She swore to me that there was nothing to
it, that there was no real romance. I would
not listen to her, and moved my things to
Sunol. She was the only woman I ever loved.

—

Once in St. Helena the local pastor came to call on Mrs. Bierce. Young Leigh ran in from the garden and remarked, Daddy, I just heard Day (my other son) say, "Damn god." The pastor and Mrs. Bierce were properly horrified, but my only comment was, "My child, how many times have I told you not to say 'Damn god' when you mean 'God damn.'"

—

Mollie Day was the prettiest girl in San Francisco—she was beautiful and kind.

—

Nothing matters, nothing matters, nothing matters.

—

A few months after I left Mrs. Bierce, Day fell in love with Eva Adkins, a girl from out in Chico. He proposed marriage. She hesitated, but he knew how to apply the pressure, and on her mother's advice, the Adkins girl finally gave in. Day applied for a license, found a minister, and invited a few guests for the wedding to be held July 22nd.

But the Adkins girl slipped out of the house by a ruse and eloped with Neil Hubbs, Day's best friend. They hopped a southbound train and were married on, you guessed it, July 22nd at French Camp. The local paper, the *Enterprise,* had a field day with it: "With a Handsomer Man! Course of True Love Runs Amuck."

Two days later the newlyweds returned, and Day greeted them at the train station.

Day had a revolver, and he used the damn thing.

Both boys began shooting, Hubbs fell mortally wounded. Then Day took a shot at Eva, shot part of her ear off. But he too had been wounded, staggered back to the hotel, crawled to his rented room, got on the bed, put another cartridge into his pistol, laid a cloth saturated with chloroform over his face, then placing the pistol to his right temple, fired it, blowing his brains out over the counterpane.

Both had begun to shoot at the same time, both died. At Sacramento the two boys parted company: Day's body was sent to St. Helena and Hubbs's to Stockton. The Adkins girl stood on the platform, one ear clipped off by the bullet, and remarked to reporters, "Now ain't that funny—one goes one way, one goes another. . . .
If anyone reading the account in the Chico *Enterprise* thinks I did wrong in marrying Hubbs at the time I did, let them consider what they would do were they a sixteen-year-old girl and placed as I was."

Day Bierce was sixteen years and eight months old.

But the newspapers weren't done with the business. My old boss at the *Argonaut,* Frank Pixley, printed an editorial asking whether the death of Day were not retribution for the father's "Bitter, heartless and unprovoked assaults. . . . Does there not rest upon his father a . . . haunting fear lest he may have transmuted to a sensitive and tender soul an inheritance which resulted in *crime* and death, while he was cultivating the gift of wounding natures just as sensitive and tender, who had not the courage to end them in murder and self-destruction?" Blah blah blah . . .

When Pixley died—sometime later, regrettably—I composed a short epitaph:

Here Lies Frank Pixley—As usual.

—

Cabbage, noun.
Reminds me.

—

. . . and then there is the matter of William Randolph Hearst, who I had only just met, it seems, around the time of all these ghastly . . . removals.

I was in my rented studio in Oakland, away from the family, when I heard a knock on the door.

I found a young man, the youngest man, it seemed to me, that I had ever confronted. His appearance, his attitude, his entire personality suggested extreme diffidence. I did not ask him in, instate him in my better chair (I had two), and inquire how we might serve each other.

If my memory is not at fault, I merely said, "Well," and awaited the result.

I am from the San Francisco *Examiner,* he exclaimed in a voice like the fragrance of violets made audible, and backed a little away.

"Oh," I said, "you come from Mr. Hearst."

Then that unearthly child lifted its blue eyes and cooed, "I *am* Mr. Hearst."

The rest is a matter of historical record. I became the "Prattler" for the princely sum of $35 a week.

Already in those days, I had been thinking over the problem of corruption in high places, and the way in which our democratic system seemed especially vulnerable in this regard. Of course, I had had some practice in this doleful study.

Back in '77 I had written of President Hayes: "Lincoln and Grant were each difficult creatures to admire, but Hayes—Hayes is only a magic lantern without even a surface to be displayed upon. You cannot see him, you cannot feel him; but you know that he extends in lessening opacity all the way from the dark side of John Sherman (the Senator from Ohio) to the confines of outer space."

And more recently—in the same vein: When a prominent industrialist, Anthony

Chabot, died I observed, "The personal property of the late Anthony Chabot of Oakland has been ordered sold. This is a noble opportunity to obtain Senator Vrooman."

No solution, political or revolutionary, is possible: majorities, embracing as they do the most ignorant, seldom think rightly; public opinion being the opinion of mediocrity is commonly a mistake and a mischief. The result is that the public writer and public speaker alike find their account in confirming the masses in their brainless errors and brutish prejudices—in glutting their omnivorous vanity and in inflaming their implacable race and national hatreds.

Patriotism is fierce as a fever, pitiless as the grave, blind as a stone, and as irrational as a headless hen.

—

M is for Moses
        who slew the Egyptian.
As sweet as a rose is
the meekness of Moses.
No monument shows his
        postmortem inscription,
but M is for Moses
        who slew the Egyptian.

—

Compulsion, noun.
The eloquence of power.

Duty, noun.
That which sternly impels us in the direction of profit, along the line of desire.

Day, noun.
A period of twenty-four hours, mostly misspent.

Things livened up a bit in early 1896; Hearst wired me from New York: "Railroad combination so strong in Washington that seems almost impossible to break them up, yet it is certainly the duty of all having interests of coast at heart to make the most strenuous efforts. Will you please go to Washington for the *Examiner*?"

I replied, "I shall be glad to do whatever I can toward defeating Mr. Huntington's Funding Bill and shall start for Washington on Monday evening next."

Collis P. Huntington was the sole surviving appendage of the Bay Area Big Four—tycoons and swindlers—that had included Mark Hopkins, Charles Crocker, and Leland Stanford, by 1896 the latter three all mercifully dead.

The Southern Pacific and Union Pacific Railroads had been built using public monies loaned out at a reasonable rate of interest. The railroad men had enriched themselves enormously, at public expense, and had failed to make anything more than token repayment of either interest or principle (an amount conservatively estimated at $75 million).

Mr. Huntington's Funding Bill was a ruse not merely intended to delay repayment for another thirty years, but in effect to assure that the issue of repayment would never be forced. The chief lobbyist for the corrupt and depraved railroad contingent in Congress was one John Boyd, whom I referred to as Huntington's tapeworm.

My first article began: Mr. Huntington is not altogether bad. Though severe, he is merciful. He tempers invective with falsehood. That is, although he says ugly things of the enemy, he has the tenderness to be careful that they are mainly lies.

—

Mr. Huntington appeared before the Committee and took his hands out of all pockets long enough to be sworn.

—

The spectacle of this old man standing on the brink of eternity, his pockets loaded with dishonest gold that he knows neither how to enjoy nor to whom to bequeath was one of the most pitiable it has been my lot to observe. He knows himself an outmate of every penal institution in the world; he deserves to hang from every branch of every tree of every state and territory penetrated by his railroads, with the sole exception of Nevada, which has no trees.

—

I called him an inflated old pigskin.

I called him a veteran calumniator.

I called him a promoted peasant.

I called him the swine of the century.

Of our modern forty thieves, Mr. Huntington is the surviving thirty-six.

—

One day I encountered Mr. Huntington on the steps of the Capitol.

Previously I had declined Huntington's hand in a committee session. It was once more offered. Met with stony rejection Huntington finally shouted, "Well, name your price; every man has a price."

My price is $75 million, and you might make it payable to my good friend, the Secretary of the Treasury.

Later on someone asked the old reptile why he had approached me. "Oh, I just wanted to see how big he was." And then added, "Now I know."

—

But that was the mauve decade. Once at the home of a western family who had recently acquired a vast fortune, I was admonished by the hostess to notice her "spinal" staircase.

—

In January 1897, the Funding Bill was defeated and I returned to San Francisco.

But I was tired of journalism; and I was getting tired of Hearst; and Hearst, in his turn, was getting tired of me. Our quarrel began over the man of the hour, and the savior proclaimed by all the Hearst papers, William Jennings Bryan.

Of whom I wrote:

Mr. Bryan's creation was the unstudied act of his own larynx; it said, Let there be Bryan and there was Bryan.

—

To the Hearst flunkies I was coming to be just an eccentric gentleman whose whim must be humored if possible, although there is no penalty if I am treated with disrespect. And I was treated with disrespect: the idiots began to edit me, me! Can you believe it?

—

Grammar, noun. A system of pitfalls thoughtfully prepared for the feet of the self-made man, along the path by which he advances to distinction.

Diaphragm, noun.
A muscular partition separating disorders of the chest from disorders of the bowels.

Dejeuner, noun.
The breakfast of an American who has been in Paris, variously pronounced.

—

My name is Boffer Bings. I was born of honest parents in one of the humbler walks of life, my father being a manufacturer of dog-oil and my mother having a small studio in the shadow of the village church where she disposed of unwelcome babes. In my boyhood I was trained to habits of industry; I not only assisted my father in procuring dogs for his vats but was frequently employed by my mother to carry away the debris of her work in the studio.

My father has, as silent partners, all the physicians of the town, who seldom wrote a prescription that did not contain what they were pleased to designate as Oil of Dog. It is really the most valuable medicine ever discovered. But most persons are unwilling to make personal sacrifice for the afflicted, and it was evident that many of the fattest dogs in town were forbidden to play with me—a fact that pained my young sensibilities, and at one time came near driving me to became a pirate....

—

My father was a deodorizer of dead dogs, my mother kept the only shop for the sale of cat's meat in my native city. They did not live happily; the difference in social rank was a chasm that could not be bridged by the vows of marriage. One morning after the customary squabbles at breakfast, my father rose from the table, quivering and pale with wrath, and proceeding to the parsonage thrashed the clergyman who had performed the marriage ceremony....

—

Resolutions of Congress, February 15, 1862. *Resolved,* That the thanks of Congress are due, and hereby tendered, to Brigadier-General Jupiter Doke and the gallant men under his command for their unparalleled feat of attacking—themselves only 2,000 strong—a Confederate army of 25,000 and utterly overthrowing it, killing 5,327, making prisoners of 19,003, of whom more than half were wounded, taking 32 guns, 20,000 stand of small arms, and, in short, the enemy's entire equipment.

Resolved, That for his unexampled victory the President be requested to designate a day of thanksgiving and public celebration of religious rites in the various churches.

Resolved, That he be requested, in further commemoration of the great event, and in reward of the gallant spirits whose deeds have added such imperishable luster to the American arms, to appoint, with the advice and consent of the Senate the following officer:

One Major-General.

Statement of Mr. Hannibal Alcazar Peyton, of Jayhawk, Kentucky.

Dat wus a almighty dark night, sho' and dese yere ole eyes ain't wuf shucks, but I's got a year like a sque'l, an' w'en I cotch de mummeer o' v'ices I knowed dat gang b'long on de far side o' de ribber. So I jes' runs in de house an' wakes Marse Doke an' tells him: "Skin outer 'dis fo' yo' life! It's de Johnny Rebs!" An' dc Lo' bress my soul! ef dat man didn' go right fru de winder in his shir'tail an' break for to cross de mule patch! An dem twenty-free hunerd mules dey jes' t'ink it is de debble hese'f wid de brandin' iron, an' dey bu'st outen dat patch like a yarth quake, an' pile inter de upper ford road, an' flash down it five deep, an' it full o' Confed'rates from en' to en'! . . .

—

Happiness, noun.
An agreeable sensation arising from contemplating the misery of another.

Hades, noun.
The place where the dead live.

Harangue, noun.
A speech by an opponent, who is known as a harangue-outang.

—

Nothing matters, nothings matters.

—

I ricocheted back and forth from one coast to the other, seeking to avoid in one what had lately most repelled me in the other.

I achieved a certain notoriety.

They began to call me the West Coast Samuel Johnson, I suppose for my Devil's Dictionary (which could not even be published under that name but was issued as *The Cynic's Wordbook*). Who but a failed critic would read anything with so lame an appellation? At any rate, if I remain unimpressed by the good Dr. Johnson,

I confess the problem lies in his definition of patriotism as "the last refuge of a scoundrel."

This is incorrect.

I beg to submit it is the first.

—

How many times, and covering a period of how many years, must one's unexplainable obscurity be pointed out to constitute fame?

Not knowing, I am almost disposed to consider myself the most famous of authors. I have pretty nearly ceased to be "discovered," but my notoriety as an obscurian [*sic*] may be said to be worldwide and apparently everlasting.

Upon the death of my second son, Leigh, who froze to death during a winter storm after an alcoholic binge, I wrote to a friend: "I am hit hard; more than you can guess—am a bit broken and gone gray of it."

—

I am leading a life of mere waiting—waiting for nothing in particular, except the end of it all. I do no work that I care to do—just the work that keeps me living—for I've no incentive, no ambition but to go on with as little friction as possible. (Why did not God make us with ball bearings?)

President Theodore Roosevelt, a man I despised for his mediocrity and warmongering, invited me to the White House.

I declined on the grounds that I never neglect old friends to make new.

This delighted Roosevelt, who promptly wrote to me: "I quite agree with you. Come tonight, and let us be old friends."

What could I do? After all, he was the President.

Presidency, noun.
The greased pig in the field game of American politics.

Things went well enough till after dinner. The President showed me the famous picture of San Juan Hill. When asked what I thought of it, I replied, "It is inaccurate since it depicts you, Mr. President, at San Juan, when in truth you were not there."

—

Hearst got it into his head to sponsor a debate at a New York hotel between two socialists, Morris Hilquitt and John Hunter, and myself. Hunter had just published a book called *Poverty* and opened the discussion with statistics. I challenged the statistics, as I would challenge all organized lies, lies organized by whatever mechanical system.

But all agreed a great deal of poverty existed. Socialism was proposed as a solution.

I said: I don't see that there is any remedy for a condition that consists in the rich being on top or, rather, the strongest being on top. They always will be.

Now don't understand me as defending that system, and I am referring to the evils of unregulated industrialism. I wish I could abolish it. I only say it is inevitable and incurable. Nothing touches me more than poverty; I have been poor myself.

In this country every man has a vote. If he is not satisfied with conditions as they are, why doesn't he change them? If the workingman and the poor are in the majority, why don't they get together? Because they haven't sense enough. They can have any laws or system they want.

The poor do not have a monopoly on all the virtues.

The general idea among the sons of discontent is that the prosperous are dishonest and the unprosperous are honest. If that is so, abolition of poverty is a nefarious business.

I don't believe in the greatest good to the greatest number—it seems to me perfect rot. I do believe in the greatest good to the best. And I would sacrifice a thousand incapable men to elevate one really good person.

Hunter said: And a dictator will bring revolution.

I said: Sure.

He said: The people alone are unconquerable.

The people, I replied, are always doing silly things. They sail in and out of great affairs, and shed a lot of blood and they are back where they were before.

He said: You think civilization has not accomplished anything in recent years. (He was smiling as he said that, the ass.)

It has accomplished everything, I said, but it has not made humanity any happier. Happiness is the only thing worth having. I find happiness in looking at poor men in the same way I do in looking at the ants in an anthill. And I find happiness in looking at the capitalist. I don't care what he does, or what the others do. It pleases me to look at them. Each man is concerned with his own happiness. Nothing matters, don't you see?

Hey, some of my best friends are socialists.

I have a socialist friend, a writer by the name of Jack London. Someone alleged to him, incorrectly, that I had said something not flattering about his work. London replied, For heaven's sake don't quarrel with Ambrose about me. He crystallized before you and I were born; and it is a magnificent crystallization.

He stopped growing a generation ago. Of course he keeps up with the newspapers, but his criteria crystallized thirty odd years ago. Had he been born a generation later, he'd have been born a socialist, and more likely an anarchist. He never reads books that aren't a hundred years old, and he glories in the fact.

—

Me, a socialist! Or an ANARCHIST!
Can you imagine it? I can't.

—

As for Hearst, when I think of him now . . . I see him: silent and smiling, he moves among men, the loneliest man. Nobody but god loves him, and he knows it; and god's love he values only insofar as he fancies that it may promote his amusing ambition to darken the door of the White House. As to that I think he would be the kind of President that this country—daft with democracy and sick with sin—is beginning to deserve.

—

I am sure it must be wrong for whole nations to be wicked. But in this worst of all possible worlds it does seem as if ethical considerations had no more weight than that to which their beauty entitles them. That may well not be, but despite the principle so dear to the hearts of the worthy gentlemen who lift protesting hands when the rights of the weak nations are invaded by strong ones, not a people on earth today has a right to be there. All have dispossessed some other people.

—

Occident, noun.
The part of the world lying west (or east) of the Orient. It is largely inhabited by Christians, a powerful subtribe of the Hypocrites, whose principle industries are murder and cheating, which they are pleased to call "war" and "commerce." These, also, are the principle industries of the Orient.

Property, noun.
Any natural thing, having no particular value, that may be held by A against the cupidity of B. Whatever gratifies the passion for possession in one and disappoints it in all others. The object of a man's brief rapacity and long indifference.

Hash, unknown.
There is no definition of the word. No one knows what hash is.

Back in Washington and Sag Harbor. Motor boating and so forth. I'm still playing at asthma. It isn't much of a game; I prefer draw poker. But asthma is cheaper.

On April 27th, 1905, Mollie E. Bierce died "of a broken heart," it is said, only a few months after divorce was granted, on the grounds of desertion.

—

Some kind soul had conveyed to her, incorrectly, of my desire for a divorce.

Mollie Day was beautiful and kind.

Nothing matters, nothing matters, nothing matters.

—

Against my better judgment I was convinced by my friend Walter Neale to assemble a collected works.

The prospectus was detailed, the work of correction and revision painstaking and difficult.

An autographed edition of all twelve volumes was bound in brown, Levantine leather, silk lined and with ornaments and lettering in twenty-two-carat gold. One hundred and twenty dollars a set. An edition deluxe.

None of my journalism was included. For the good reason that I have always despised the whole damn enterprise.

The reviews were what you would expect: "A depressing assemblage of worn-out and fly-blown stuff. Except from the upholsterer's point of view they are not books at all" (H. L. Mencken).

"Potatoes set in platinum" (Wilson Follett).

"Turnips in Tiffany's window" (Richard O'Connor).

—

We think in words. We cannot think without them. Shallowness or obscurity of speech means shallowness or obscurity of thought.

To feel rightly one must think and know rightly. Cabbage, noun. . . .

—

After the debacle of my collected works, I got restless.

I got restless, read about the situation in Mexico; looks like a real fight; it's about time; I've corresponded with this Carranza fellow, and I like him; I've decided to go down to Juarez and view the scene for myself.

—

O, Lawyer Tum Suden,
I beg you'll be quiet:
Don't always be broodin'
On causes of riot.

For any poor sinner
To nature a debtor
A salad for dinner
With peace is far better,

The Sacred Affiant
Is careful to mention
Than any stalled client
And therewith contention.

So stop your intrudin'
On sluggers, I say,
O, Lawyer Tum Suden
Tum Duden, Tum Day.

—

Had a lot of letters to write before my departure.

To a young admirer (Nellie Stickler): We shall never meet, so let me offer a little advice.

Well . . .

But you are happy, and that is all that it is worth to be. Nothing else is of any value—just happiness. The difference between a good person and a bad one is that one finds happiness in goodness; the other in badness;

but consciously or unconsciously, happiness is all they seek or can seek. Even self-sacrifice is a species of self-indulgence. And at the end of it we see that nothing matters.

To Mollie E. Day . . .

—

Picture, noun.
A representation in two dimensions of something wearisome in three.

—

Resident, noun.
Unable to leave.

Talk, verb transitive.
To commit an indiscretion without temptation, from an impulse without purpose.

—

To my daughter, Helen, January 27th, 1913:

Dear Bib, You are well provided for, and my proofreading stunt—four years of it—is over. In America you can't go East or West anymore, or North, the only avenue of escape is South. I'm going back to Washington and make preparations to leave. I'll take some letters with me and strike the border near El Paso. It will be easy enough to get along. I'm going to buy a donkey and hire a peon. I can see what's doing; perhaps write a few articles about the situation; and then pass to the west coast of Mexico. From there I can go to South America, cross the Andes and ship to England. This fighting in Mexico interests me. I want to go down there and see if these Mexicans can shoot straight.

—

Dear Mollie . . .

Death marked me at Kennesaw
Mountain . . .

Ah, how beautiful she is! He springs forward with extended arms. As he is about to clasp her, he feels a stunning blow upon the back of his neck; a blinding white light blazes all about him with a sound like the shock of a cannon—then all is darkness and silence.

Peyton Farquhar is dead; his body, with a broken neck, swings gently from side to side beneath the timbers of the Owl Creek Bridge.

All this we see.

Fade to black.

End of play.

—

CODA

Applause, noun.
The echo of a platitude.

Critic, noun.
A person who boasts himself hard to please because nobody tries to please him.

—

Congratulation, noun.
The civility of envy.

—

End of play (again).

Psychology; or, Bring a Weasel and a Pint of Your Own Blood

Psychology was commissioned by Stuck Pigs Squealing of Melbourne, Australia (artistic director, Chris Kohn), and received a workshop production at Stanford University under the direction of Matt Moore in 2006.

This demented play is for the three Lemurvians: Erin Courtney, Karinne Keithley, and Kate Ryan.

NOTE

The occasional appearance of an asterisk in the middle of a speech indicates that the next speech begins to overlap at that point. The overlapping speeches are all clearly marked in the text.

A
candle in the dark.

A
GIRL *face appears in a small window quite high above, a window within a golden frame and perhaps above the frame strange, illustrated double-somethings that could be ears or horns.*

Under her breath she mutters something (we do not hear), something snide and cutting, but alas we cannot hear.

Downstage far left is the GUY *and his* GREEN CAR. *(The* GREEN CAR *is simply a green wooden chair with another guy dressed in black (à la Bunraku) sitting in it. But according to the wonder of theater, we think* GREEN CAR. *The* GIRL*'s snide remarks are meant, obviously, for these two.*

Pause of what the hell was that.

She mutters under her breath once more.

The GUY *prickles, stiffens.*

She does the bad thing again.

Again he prickles, stiffens.

GUY:
Come down here and say that.

She looks disdainfully at him and his GREEN CAR.

GUY:
You heard me. You heard me. Come down here and say that. Come on down here and say that.

She does the raspberry.

The GUY *stiffles and prickens and looks at his* CAR. *His* CAR *prickles and stiffens and looks at his* GUY.

She does the raspberry.

She does the raspberry again.

GUY: *(under his breath)*
Okay, okay, you can just go and do that that bad thing. Go ahead.

She does an exceptional raspberry.

GUY: *(under his breath)*

Okay, okay, you have made your point. I guess you sure have. *(aloud)* Come on. Come on down here and do that.

She does the bad thing once more.

GUY:

Come on down here and do that.

She does the bad thing once more.

GUY:

Come on down here and do that.

She mimes doing but does not do the bad thing, catching him off balance thereby.

GUY:

What do you call that?

She indicates, what do you mean?

GUY:

What do you call that thing that that you do?

She indicates: you are a colossal dunce.

GUY:

Do you, er, do you have have some kind of a name for that thing that you do or is it is it maybe just some kind of a some kind of a thing that you make up sorta on the spot sorta?

She mimics, on the spot sorta.

Another pause of what the hell.

The GUY *looks at the* GREEN CAR*; the* GREEN CAR *looks at the* GUY.

△ *Someone or two or three recites one of the mangled propositions of Euclid:*

> A chain the same air line of the way can be persecuted, through the connection of both points that does not specify her.

The GUY *stiffens, prickles.*

The GREEN CAR *stiffens, prickles.*

The GIRL *smiles sweetly, then mocks as best she can the way they stiffen and prickle.*

(We notice for the first time that the GREEN CAR *possesseth feet.*

The GUY *tries to ignore what we have all noticed for the first time, namely, this fact of* GREEN CAR *feet.)*

She does the Prong.

She does the Hook and Ladder.

She does the Double Prong.

GUY:

Okay, okay, you just go and. You just go and.
You just come on down here and do that.
You just come on down here and do that.
You just come on down here and do that.

She indicates that she cannot hear what he is saying.

GUY:

Okay, okay, you just go and. You just go and.
You just come on down here and do that.
You just come on down here and do that.
YOU JUST COME ON DOWN HERE AND DO THAT.

She indicates that she STILL cannot hear what he is saying.

He despairs.

The GREEN CAR *tries to console him.*

The GIRL *mocks in turn, his despair and his inward raging.*

Door of high window slams shut slams open. She shrieks.

GIRL:

I seen you beat your kid.

I heard you say my kid was a loser.

I heard you say my kid was a noser.

I seen you beat your kid with sticks.

I heard you say my kid was a dumb doggo.

I seen you beat your kid with a piece of wood with nails sticking out.

I heard you say my kid was a dead monkey.

I seen you I seen you I seen you do dat and dat and dat.
Dat dat dat.

Pause of wondering what the hell is dat.

GUY:

Go to, ah, got to, ah, go to, ah, merde.

She is astonished by this.

GUY:

Go to, ah, merde.

She is enthralled.

GUY:

Go to, ah, merde.

She is in love. Closes (the little) door above. Appears as if by sortilege below, through another (normal) door opened by a strange DWARF *who wears a golden fez who has been also reciting the stage directions as though they were commands.*

She stands there, ready.

~

She stands there ready, but nothing much happens.

The people pick up various tools and begin to tackle a variety of tasks that at first glance appear to be a part of a scene change but in reality are not. They are merely random and pointless acts of barely plausible, pseudoconstruction: these include the hammering in and pulling out of nails with a large claw hammer; the unbolting and bolting of clasps and turnbuckles; the unfurling and hanging of pointless and unnecessary drapery; the stacking and unstacking of chairs and platforms, cinder blocks, and whatever else is to be found. All of this is to be accomplished with the greatest patience, silence, and cunning, and apparent technical purposefulness of the theater.

The DWARF, *who now wears a black fez, directs all of this, snapping his fingers and making low grunts.*

As the GIRL *begins slowly to disrobe in the half-light, a creepy, shapeless, and unconvincing sock puppet appears within the precinct of her former window. This puppet is disturbing because he bears no resemblance to any known creature. Except one: the weasel.*

Is she going to speak for the weasel? Is the weasel going to speak for her? Neither, as it transpires.

SOCK PUPPET *does a vast armadillo of a raspberry.*

This so distracts us that we do not notice that the GUY *has been replaced by the partially clad* GIRL. *Guess what has become of the one* (GUY) *who has been so egregiously and unconvincingly sworn at?*

WEASEL (GUY):

Your kid throwed a ball at my kid.

GIRL:

You you you. You no good cabbage.
Come down here and say that.

WEASEL (GUY):

Your brother flashed my sister.
Your brother flashed my mother.
Your brother flashed the Pope.
Your brother flashed Mrs. Sprinkle.
Your brother is a dumb doggo.
Your brother has shit for brains.
Your brother has just got down from the trees.*

Your brother flashed my sister.
Your brother flashed my mother.

Your brother flashed the Pope.
Your brother flashed Mrs. Sprinkle.
Your brother is a dumb doggo.
Your brother has shit for brains.
Your brother has just got down from the trees.

GIRL:

Oh yeah? Oh yeah? Oh yeah? Oh yeah?
Oh yeah? Oh yeah? Oh yeah?
Come down here and say that.
Come down here and say that.
Come down here and say that.
Come down here and say that.
Come down here and say that.
Come down here and say that.

This sweet (but unconvincing) exchange is repeated word for word exactly the same dumb as the hole in the donut nine hundred times. The GREEN CAR *looks back and forth from horrid* SOCK PUPPET *to horrid* GIRL *and cannot decide which is more embarrassing. Finally, the* GIRL *stops and mutters to herself while the* SOCK PUPPET *repeats twice more for effect his screed.*

A pause of accusatory burnout.

Another.

An electric RAT *scuttles along the far wall.*

All watch this, curious only to see whether the damn thing malfunctions;

it (ratly) does or doesn't;

silence. Pause. Silence.

▲ *Someone or two or three recites another of the mangled propositions of Euclid:*

> The pagination of the right of the chain can extensively be indefinite in a same air line of the chain.

She gives the SOCK PUPPET *the finger.*

The SOCK PUPPET *rages inwardly.*

She does the Prong.

The SOCK PUPPET *sizzles.*

She does the Double Prong.

The SOCK PUPPET *stiffens.*

She does the Triple Prong.

The SOCK PUPPET *stiffens and prickles.*

She does the Monkey Brain.

The SOCK PUPPET *quivers with intense hatred.*

She does the Sicilian mal'occhio . . .

The SOCK PUPPET *puts on a small red fez and speaks coldly.*

WEASEL (GUY):
  Why the moustaches?

The GIRL *is puzzled as she possesseth no moustaches.*

GIRL:

So? So? So what?

WEASEL (GUY):

So why the moustaches?

GIRL:

. . .

WEASEL (GUY):

Pourquoi les moustaches?

GIRL:

Oh, and aren't we sophisticated?

WEASEL (GUY):

Why the moustaches?

GIRL:

So? So what's the implication?

WEASEL (GUY):

Why the moustaches?

GIRL:

"Why the moustaches?" What's that supposed to mean?

WEASEL (GUY): *(cold and dead)*

Why. The. Moustaches?

GIRL:

So?

WEASEL (GUY):

So. Why the moustaches?

GIRL:

"Why the moustaches?" What's that supposed to mean?

WEASEL (GUY):

Pourquoi les moustaches?

GIRL:

. . .

WEASEL (GUY):

Pourquoi les moustaches?

GIRL:

. . .

WEASEL (GUY):

POURQUOI LES MOUSTACHES!

The GIRL turns away and rages inwardly.

The SOCK PUPPET surveys his vast domain with triumph and withdraws to his inner sanctum and carefully closes the little door behind him.

On the door is painted the face of the SUN avec moustaches.

The GIRL turns on the GREEN CAR, who sensing a palpable threat tries to make herself very, very small.

GIRL:

What the hell are you looking at?

GREEN CAR, *sensing a palpable threat, tries to make herself even smaller.*

GIRL:

You're looking at me like I was an immigrant. You're looking at me like I was a foreigner. I don't like it when people stare, when people go and stare at you like you just came down from the trees. You think I have a tail? Take a good look. I don't have a tail. My people never had tails. My people are of an unimpeachable origin. We once lived among the blue bells. Not in the treetops like monkey brains there.

Indicating the now-closed window high above, now sun now moon.

A hopeless pause of rancor and unease.

Pause. Silence. Pause.

Something happens in a far corner of the theater. Something barely visible, something barely audible.

GIRL: *(softly)*

I had a little dog once who looked like you. Yes, just like you. I would call and he would come running. Sometimes he would come running even though I hadn't called. Don't know why. Maybe he could tell there was something the matter. Maybe he could tell there was something the matter even before I could.

I think this life is truly awful. A dog's life. Doggo the dog. Just when you think you have things figured out, they go pop and just change on you and you not a whit the wiser. People act strange and are always doing things that don't make any sense. Most people—face the fact—act like they have no soul. People without souls.

GREEN CAR *is now listening carefully. Perhaps this is what* GREEN CAR *has been thinking all along himself, herself, whichever.*

GIRL: *(softly)*

You ever do something really nice for someone. You know. You invite them for dinner on your birthday and prepare them the Pascal feast of roasted lamb and they and they don't show and stand you up and you are shaking with rage and sorrow and disbelief and the knowledge of the sheer futility of ever knowing what is going on inside another person's head. You hear yourself saying, Lowell, Lowell, you creep . . .

But you are not speaking, because you are only raging inwardly and the voice you hear is the voice of yourself raging inwardly. Psychology. Psychology. I mean, take a good look at people. Liars. Cheats. Just a bunch of conniving con artists. Frauds. Hacks. Losers. Nosers. Losers like Lowell. You cannot imagine how low they can sink and how desperate and opportunistic they are, all of them. How simple-minded and callous and just plain spiritually empty.

A dog is better than any person. A dog is not like a person. I hate them all. People without souls.

I won't tell you what happened to my little dog.

Something bad, something very bad. He was only a mutt.

Bitten on the neck.

Just a little mutt.

Bitten on the neck by a *(whisper)* weasel.

Psychology. Psychology is just a . . . an empty word.

The psychology of Lowell blah blah—what does she mean?

So what does he mean?

So what does what mean?

Ha. The word. *Psychology.*

The GREEN CAR *finds the existential predicament described here just as much of a puzzle of entrapment as does the half-clad* GIRL.

As the GIRL *slowly and awkwardly gets dressed, we hear the first Procession of Knights from Wagner's* Parsifal: *"We bear the grail in concealing shrine to its holy place; whom have you in that gloomy shrine that you mourning hither bear?"*

Various shadowy figures collect and continue as before the random and pointless redistribution of things, stuff, junk. Most of the things this time end up in a heap to one side. Stage right maybe.

▼ *Someone or two or three recites yet another of Euclid's (mangled) prepositions, as the insane* DWARF, *who now wears a white fez, mutters and snaps his finger directing as before the random and pointless scene change.*

If the right pagination to the given
cancellation, a totality can be
persecuted, with using the way that the startings
and an obstruction
indicate that the center.

Silence. Pause. Silence.

Slowly, the door of the little window opens and we see with horror a GREEN CAR PUPPET, *faceless and horrid like the grill of an antique automobile from a depraved and former time. The* GREEN CAR PUPPET *is mic'd and speaks with a cold and deadly quietness.*

GREEN CAR PUPPET:

You know what you are, yes, you know . . .

Which one of us is he referring to? they both wonder, the GIRL *and the* GUY, *the former now seated in* GREEN CAR'S GREEN CHAIR.

GUY:

—

GIRL:

?

GREEN CAR PUPPET:

You, yeah you . . .

GUY:

—

GIRL:

?

GREEN CAR PUPPET:

You, yeah you . . .

GUY:

Yeah?

GREEN CAR PUPPET:

You're a passive aggressive hostile fuck.

GUY:

Oh yeah?

GREEN CAR PUPPET:

Yeah . . .

GUY:

Come on,* come on down here . . .

GIRL:

Come on down here and say that.

GREEN CAR PUPPET:

Yeah?

GUY AND GIRL:

Yeah.

GREEN CAR PUPPET:

You know what you are?

GUY:

Yeah?

GREEN CAR PUPPET:

You're a passive aggressive hostile fuck.

GUY:

Oh yeah?

GREEN CAR PUPPET:

Yeah . . .

GUY:

Come on,* come on down here . . .

GIRL:

Come on down here and say that.

GREEN CAR PUPPET:

Yeah?

GUY AND GIRL:

Yeah.

This exchange is repeated as though on a tape loop word for word exactly the same dumb as the hole in a donut nine hundred times. The GIRL *in the* GREEN CHAIR *and the* GUY *look at each other both bristling with inner rage.*

Something happens once more in a far corner of the theater. Something barely visible, something barely audible.

All crane their necks, curious and distracted.

There is something about this egregious rubbernecking that is repellant, almost obscene.

~

The darkness darkens. Are we going blind?

The DWARF, *lurking in the gathering shadows, has some kind of fit, or conniption, or episode, and he is writhing on the floor making little noises and worse.*

All quietens.

All quietens, except for.

All quietens, except for?

All quietens, except for a tapping that once more inaugurates the random and pointless nailing, unnailing, unbolting and bolting up, and stacking up of lumber, and unrolling and rolling of drapes and curtains and all the rest of this random and pointless business. All of this is as before directed by the DWARF, *who has apparently recovered from his conniption and fit and episode, and perhaps inwardly one secretly wonders if perhaps he is not directing anything and that the activity is not being directed by anyone and anything but is simply happening in the way a candle burns and burns until he is nothing but a glop of goop, a shapeless glop of melted wax.*

▼ *:: Someone or Something or two or three recite the last of Euclid's mangled propositions:*

> All the right angles are in the agreement.
> If two chains are persecuted, this cut the
> third place.

We are distracted by this. The lights do something that they should not, and we are back where we were (roughly) at the beginning, if we can remember back that far. We hear muttering:

> (What the hell does that mean?)
>
> (What mean?)
>
> ("A whit the wiser.")

The GIRL *opens the door.*

GIRL:
> It is a concept from psychology.

The GIRL *shuts the door.*

GUY:
> ?

GREEN CAR: *(back where he was) . . .*

The GIRL *opens the door.*

GIRL:

But a dunce like you wouldn't know about psychology.

The GIRL *shuts the door.*

GUY:

Psychology.* What . . .

GREEN CAR:

What does psychology have to do with it?

The GIRL *opens the door.*

GIRL:

. . . idiot . . .

The GIRL *shuts the door.*

GUY AND GREEN CAR:

Come down here and say that.

The GIRL *opens the door.*

GIRL:

. . . moron . . .

The GIRL *shuts the door.*

GUY AND GREEN CAR:

Come down here and say that.

The GIRL *opens the door.*

GIRL:

…imbecile…

The GIRL *smiles and shuts the door—now wearing the face of a silvery moon.*

GUY AND GREEN CAR:

Come on down here and say that.
Come on down here and say that.
Come on down here and say that.
Come on down here and say that.
Come on down here and say that.
Come on down here and say that.
Come on down here and say that.

The door remains shut and does not therefore open.

They wait (stupidly) for the door to open.

GUY:

Psychology. Ha. What.* Who.

GREEN CAR:

Psychology. Fifty-cent word.

We first see then hear the DWARF *(with his first golden fez) lead a funeral procession and once more hear very quietly the music from* Parsifal: *"We bear the grail in concealing shrine to its holy place; whom have you in that gloomy shrine that you mourning hither bear?"*

In the procession we see a flower-strewn casque that bears the name of Woofli.

Darkness.

Pause. Silence. Pause.

We hear a violin.

We hear muttering.

We hear a plucked string.

We hear light, silvery laughter.

Blackout.

End of play.

A Morphology of Small Errors, and Catalogue of the Cahoonery of Moths and Spiders

A Morphology of Small Errors is a libretto in development at the Theater of a Two-Headed Calf, with music by Brendan Connelly.

SETTING

A location as such; a place set as so; a place beginning to be one of the, after the; a place beginning to be one after another of these; dubious: a house in the woods.

Quiet.

ACT ONE

> An awful spider. A person
> Lara. Laura. Moira.

SCENE ONE
The Moron of errors appears and not to.

SCENE TWO
A spider is tempted, too.

SCENE THREE
Lara and Laura are an in between the.
An a; an o.

SCENE FOUR
Cahoonery.

SCENE FIVE
Seventy-three small mortgaged suitcases may come to to to ah. Arrive at the.

SCENE SIX
Awe.

SCENE SEVEN
Safety.

SCENE EIGHT
A plank.

SCENE NINE
Awe ways won woe. Hwaet.

SCENE TEN
Wrong.

SCENE ELEVEN
Awe ways won woe. Wrong that.

SCENE TWELVE
A.

SCENE THIRTEEN
Awe ways woe won.

SCENE FOURTEEN
The fly spiders and they
are a spider of a of of a

fly. A person a a. A
a. Continental bee
and peeps the Spiders
all cahooned and to
Morpho for Moth.

SCENE FIFTEEN
Yea.

SCENE NOT FIFTEENATTATTAGGATTATAKALUZA
Algebra.

SCENE SIXTEEN
Deleted and . . .

SCENE SEVENTEEN
An error very small with a nose like the.

Pause for reflection.

SCENE EIGHTEEN
The chorus approaches disguised as a.

SCENE NINETEEN
Signage.

SCENE TWENTY
Is an as is; goat's.

SCENE TWENTY-ONE
Jackson.

SCENE TWENTY-TWO
A song of the Moth People. Go Moth go.

SCENE TWENTY-THREE

Awe eaw
Wae wea
Ewa and. A cannot
may not follow to a
Not can who to can?

SCENE TWENTY-FOUR

Old Windy Gap.
(Kicks the pony's ass):
Get thee home; thou egg of bastardy—!

SCENE TWENTY-FIVE

Near the coincidental error that is
two plus three.
Algol.
No. Not
a.

SCENE 26

Morula.

SCENE 27

Lara and Laura. A sighting signifies
the scene in question.

SCENE 28

Someone shuffles the deck.

SCENE 29

Shuffles and reshuffles and cuts the deck.

SCENE 30
Swoo. Lara and Laura
swore
a morula
and the shoe
fits.

SCENE 31
Go, foo of shits, thy sway.

SCENE 32
A toad and a bat and a bumblebee.

~

Snows rise up on Fear Mountain we
had not such a picture and a er a an.

. . .

SCENE 33
Invents the weasel and works her wheel.
Red bird.
Moira.
Fate.
String.
Habitual Joe and
Lara and Laura they
too to go are
digged.
And
a
Man walks to the edge
of the.

SCENE 34

Hare thinks better of the whole

. . .

SCENE

Tep

(Go Tep, go—!)

SCENE TIP

. . .

Go Tep, go—!

THIRTY-FIVE

It.

Pause for time to think the matter out.

Ends

badly. Hardly, but badly.

SCENE 36

An epic sight of dark houses and people

in the.

SCENE 37

Me-ti speaks to us softly so so softly we cannot

. . .

Lara and Laura can't.

SCENE 39

A forest hides the big green

rabbit.

SCENE 40

Is not really Scene 40 it is

SCENE 41

There is a catch and the. To
a. Someone is who
scratches their. Hat. Head.
Foot. Thy. Lemurian.
Red bird. A a. A a. A
phpooph.

INTERMISSION: SANDWICH MAN WITH SANDWICH BOARDS

~

. . .

SCENE 42

Forty degrees of frost. Chiseled crows. Sky
might.
Resolved, that.
Awe. Woe.
Ice
Toe.

SCENE 43

Mortal sin is a man who not to see
is not to been
seen. His. In a
cup. Red bird cake.
Red
tongue long as the Moravian
banner.
Star.
Dust storms.
Whirls whirls whirls. Out
here.

SCENE 44
Devils cherno play with eldness a clothes with no people
in them.
Chort.
Chert.
What is that?

SCENE 45
Blown top of blown day a jubilee
why why a
system of bugs.
Entered. Entered in to.
Et in arcadia ego.
Ago. An
hour as in Morocco Morton's
private account.

. . .

SCENE 46
Errors abounding in the Cattattatta. Cattattatta.

SCENE 47
Cross out all 46s. Cross them
up ulp out.

SCENE 48
Awe ways woe won.

SCENE 49
A chorus of something lost sings the chorus of the
lost one.

50

Um. Lara and Laura and Moira.
They fall out all under a. A
thought threes them. All out of
line, and into an um.
Scene done in by her undoigt
um.
Scene 50 done um.

End of Act I (Herringsredwingdoo!)

ACT II

Tep tips off Tip who taps Tup for a.

SCENE ONE

Old cat with Egyptian profile old old oldy
suffers from "repressed rage."

SCENE TWO

Morpho becomes.

SCENE THREE

Morpho morpho becomes a dot.

SCENE FOUR

Lara and Laura. And Moira.

SCENE FIVE

Moira runs

SCENE SIX

From a dot at far left to another dot
on far right and all

SCENE SEVEN
Dots in between.

SCENE EIGHT
In between each another one.

SCENE NINE
In between a dot and another another
appears and between on both sides
appears another dot and. In between
both sides and the dot adjacent
appears another dot.
And between the. Between
that and the fallen. Tower
and the. Moon
and between that and. Between
that and the fallen. Tower
and the moon. Between
and between the. Between
and between the. Between
and between the. Between
that and the fallen. Tower
and the moon. Between
and between the. Between
and between the. Between
and between the. Between
that and the fallen. Tower
and the moon. Between
all dots more dots. Dots
between dots.
As Moira disposes.

SCENE TEN
Moira smiles as the as the moon
spiders and moths
tip off tep.

SCENE ELEVEN
Does Tep arise and does he
topped off
arrive? Nobody knows.
The the Morpho knows
the Morpho know not
the.

SCENE TWELF
Under a a rock tis a tis a is a Moth it.
Luna tick.

SCENE THIRTEEN
Lara and Laura look at a far

SCENE FOURTEEN
Mock rock. Tock
Tuck.

SCENE FIFTEEN
Laura and yes. Lara and her they
are to do the look
at. The far the.
Moira smiles.

SCENE 16
Light is a cutting noise is a sharp
it is as
a Moira a

smiles unknown
to knowing.

~

SCENE
Crunch.

SCENCE
Crunk.

SCCENCC
Crun.

SCCCNCC
Crunk. Of and of a not till to tip to
a Lara
like. Laura.
Moira.
Now as as a Red Bird. Monsoor Redwingerp.

~

SCENE OMEGA: the notorious Duck-Rabbit disappears at Silvery midnight behind the the Moon's favorite hat. Footprints in the

wet oh wet

Silvery nightgrass. Ss. Ss.

End.

The Invention of Tragedy

The Invention of Tragedy has been in several workshops since 2005, all under the direction of Ken Rus Schmoll, at New York University's Write Act program and at Classic Stage Company. Thanks to the Corporation of Yaddo and the MacDowell Colony. Thanks also to the Write Act program at NYU and to the Classic Stage Company, Brian Kulick, artistic director.

NOTE

The occasional appearance of an asterisk in the middle of a speech indicates that the next speech begins to overlap at that point. The overlapping speeches are all clearly marked in the text.

The Invention of Tragedy by the chorus of students, all alike and all unalike, at _________ School in _________ City in the State of New _________. There are 1,001 of them, and they are trying like the devil to tell a simple story. Perhaps the story about the tragedy of the SANDWICH MAN with sandwich boards on which nothing is written and hence with nothing to say.

Perhaps there are not 1,001 of them, things being what they are. Perhaps there are fewer kids; perhaps there are some adults scattered discreetly here and there. All are seated politely on benches and risers in a large (theatrical) space. But if there are fewer people, the remainder of the chorus may be made up of rows and rows of dolls, mannequins, objects, pieces of lumber, and so forth.

SCENE ≳ : CATACHRESIS CATATASTICAL

FIRST CHORUS:

And chop the chails off all cats. All things come all things come and are based on the hope apple. Let there be hope apples, hope apples, and donuts of every silvery degree. Let there be a dragon of trees and of washing without washcloths bags cats wardrobes bungle things and other things traps and twerps and words and greater words of estuarial conviviality. La la la la la la la. La la la.

Pause.

A penlight comes up on one of them, one just as alike and unalike as can be, only she is smaller and more intense than the rest. She is not therefore the same and is different.

This difference is a problem.

This difference is a problem for one and all as we shall see the problem will not go away.

Silence as all bend low to consider her.

Pause.

Er, she goes. Er. All back to where they was.

SECOND CHORUS:

And chop the chails off all cats. The bird of alignment off to nuts grows grows a possum hell bore can't do finger whole of a part yessir yessir yessiree at to on an island scamper way to benumbed fruitcake walk to lean to adventure whose whose which of the parterre o glad-eyed speak, er, speech and say not to nothing but hinge grammaticus grammarye's red boast o machine o machine break down de doom. O machine of the other the other imagining.

Pause. Something wrong with this. A doubt crosses briefly each brow.

THIRD CHORUS:

O sanctuary girl be not too to yourself at an ashcan drama out of the squabble fleecy flacco fleecy flocculent huge bitten dogcat a thing warped in HELIOS pardon the digital wind nut gutter hat implosion o o swing thou sleepy head. And chop the chails off all cats. And chop the chails off all cats. Doggy doggy of prolix helix gone to trombone city on the way all the way to the erp.

FOURTH CHORUS:

Three full stops beyond Seti Osiris we mean o o his saurian Ahura Mazda domino domononatonatomorpho morpho pie hat pie tree forest of whisperz and whimperz on the trellis of Egypt her hat who found his bed out out past the o blushbluishngreenbedslipper park where no one has no one has to look at what is not worth the trouble and ho they go ho ho hoot and hoo like a what it is what does that mean damn meant you mean no no yes yes. And chop the chails off all cats.

A pause of inappropriate dogginess.

FIFTH CHORUS:

O mighty minimax whereby of the full flower all rings doth make the pseudocrocodile arise and knuckled be and thus left to lift all shoes to an an o pied piper of care. Care for the fabled donuts of silvery and telephone and obsolete feet. Ink and the bars across the windows minds hearts and theaters of an IDEA. Hope full duck. And chop the chails off all cats. Path through a time crammed into exposure with scales of gold and buttons and bottle caps. Time goes. Flees. Rents and drills. So so so and to where are the arrows feathering feathering fletch. An inch too too near the can of can not. Tells a stop to stop to on to not's airy star can and an end so is the true imagined.

Pause and another of choral anxiety and er. She goes to the dark, and someone lights a candle.

SIXTH CHORUS:

Latin corset shall aspire aspiration to be ah whatever is up to there hey heh hey heh hey heh hey heh heh by and o that personal candle to toe toe to candle to toe toe to candle as an outdoor answer to the matter [ANSWERER: Er,] to the matter of what. And chop the chails off all cats. And as the gift fly goes up up into a ton of flammable water ghost ghosting to o tower being cave of boy and girl reputation so. In the character of a wish. In the character of an act. In the character of a group of people onepeopleundergod all sing all saying ding aling ding dong the same damn thing aling. Ding done din.

A suspicious toe of someone suspicious emerges briefly and then disappears just as suspiciously.

Silence.

All pretend to not notice the. Er, unlawfulness. Fracture in the er.

Time and space a.

SEVENTH CHORUS:

Cry out and flup cry out and flip up to that ATTIS banjo ant bear this time hold on hot bear with they open paw of carry to whom the hot honey. O gluey o. And chop the chails off all cats. O o see not with cannot to the brink of a Caroline tablecloth and go to Tuesday with more wood than before the fire Monday strange and the grip of rotor incline and of ramp concept as you yes as you* break all the all glassy world upon the head doggy doggy doggy is a poor cat that shuffles known to be an item cast into the sky qua sky dog qua dog mouth qua mouse fur the color of the.

A wine of glass with redwing red wine in her shatters somewhere a flagrant gless of red mess hell.

Shattered pause to consider an instance of breakage unknown unknown unknownable.

FIRST SHATTERED CHORUS:

Glass who who broke thee who. And chop the chails off all cats. Who?

Silence as of a wind of other worlds.

We see the unlawful shadow of two cat's ears proceed across the whole world.

SECOND SHATTERED CHORUS:

Who. Who?

Pause nothing pause the.

EIGHTH CHORUS:

Morpho morpho Morpho and and who. This it it it can do and be kissed too if an answer comes calling at the which door that who was. Okay. Okay? Or hey hay straw hay to who and a restitution of the one who brings the good child home in the red wagon of slats and push cushions touched by who. And chop the chails off all cats. Who? By long-knuckled death. Morpho o morph morpho. Who. And chop the chails off all cats. Who? The great worm must carry the day and not because of whose identity has concluded with catastrophe and. For. For each market must race home under a cloud of day ruin night's skate of shakes and palsy.

NINTH CHORUS:

Qua Qualitative qua reluctant human person er man and horsey do observe the moon from each cananadadaddaan. To thee the soap hath to be up to under the killer's garage. Car knowledge offering. Goose ascending in tall ascent to please the St. Elmer's fire. Ridicule and plausible steeples on the way. Er. Go thou to that house and allowance for a dry catch hatch make cooling cooking as the biggest steam table clank clears all off to wages contractual on the broken-down shoebox back of the poor. Who. And chop the chails off all cats. Who? Pour poor pour. Poor yous.

A something strange happeneth.

—

ONE steps forth from the mess of the rest. Guess who the one whose toe violated the unknown zone before. One step steps forth from the rest. Unlawfulness is revealed. Awfulness.

In her awfulness, this is the ANSWERER.

An axe appears in the hands of a distant OTHER one who is not a little surprised by this.

Pause.

Silence.

Pause.

CHORUS: *(fractured)*

Horror horror horror the world is broken broken and come to be fractured.

To which the ANSWERER *replies:*

ANSWERER:

I am here to announce, er. I am her to er here to pronounce and enounce and denounce and renounce a total that is TOTAL expostulation of cats er. A total exposure of cats er. A TOTAL I mean TOTAL departure of cats.

She steps gingerly one step farther.

I mean I am here to announce and PROCLAIM a departure of all cats.

Far down the line by the OTHER *one with the axe the* ENFORCER *now steps forth.*

This is the ENFORCER *of the choral consensus as ramified by the Supreme Court of the state of New* _________.

The ANSWERER *takes a few more steps out. We see that she has attacked er attached to her behind what is supposed to be some kind of tail.*

She turns to examine her tail, turns back.

Alas alas.

As a tail it is not completely convincing.

Details, details. Steps one step farther.

CHORUS: *(further fractured)*

Awfulness. Unlawfulness. Horror horror o horror.

ANSWERER:

A TOTAL and RANDOM departure of cats.

CHORUS: *(yet more fractured)*

Awful.

An awful pause.

ENFORCER:

Give me that axe.

CHORUS:

?

ENFORCER:

That axe. The one there.

The AXE PERSON *gives the axe to the* ENFORCER.

The AXE PERSON *is glad to be rid of the horrid thing.*

The axe is very large and very. The ENFORCER *slowly drags the axe across the whole world.*

ANSWERER:

I have had had at this time to take the step to er this point some yards off and say something er the same thing again.

CHORUS:

?

ENFORCER:

This is an axe. Your saucy has caused the sky to to become dark and covered with moss and of murk the deepest.

ANSWERER:

I care not the axe who.

ENFORCER:

Axe can cause trouble.

ANSWERER:

I have become one for my own mind in thought. I perceive how cats have been mistreated in these parts. Fed with crap food. Despised and chased. Played cat in the bag with and other such. Dull the fur. I see them treed and often hopeless and puzzled. And then there is is the oft-spoken threat of top er chop off the chails of. Er them.

ENFORCER:

This is you're a doing does a rupture. A chorus must speak as one. Your doing ruptures the balloon. Agree to come back. We speak as one. You outside yourself in law. Wind shall speak the darkest.

ANSWERER:

O give a fart. I shall stay and restay.

ENFORCER:

Wind shall speak. As one we chirchirrrup to dooms. Dooms,
I say.

ANSWERER:

I give voice to that catalogue of being you have caused to labor and distress with threats of chop the tail off of. Pfaff.

ENFORCER:

Pfui in reply. You and your wit is a hidden in a foul trench of Mister Toad.

ANSWERER:

Pfaff. The catafalque gives much my voice strong pitch to care and er ear.

ENFORCER:

Return and we will consider a political act on the cat problem.

ANSWERER:

Too late. I am free.

ENFORCER:

See this axe.

ANSWERER:

Too late. I am beyond the fear place.

ENFORCER:

A chorus must speak with one voice. By Zaa. By Altoona. By what the wind creaks on Crazy Day. What good is another chorus to be if not to do this thing here?

ANSWERER:

Too late. I am free.

ENFORCER:

See this axe.

ANSWERER:

Too late.

ENFORCER:

See this axe?

Macrurous pause of feline strangeness.

TENTH CHORUS:

So to table the hedge before the conflagration synod hatches a pea. Pop roar sauce ship dish tight thin path this bathe you cut urge valve with yes zebra size. And leave uncut the cat tails some uncut of the lesser catapults yet un. Uncut vision about item an edible gallop circus. Valor follows the children of night into previous celebration as the wing watches all over the roar. And of ear the innumerable pairs. Pour pour.

ELEVENTH CHORUS:

To not guest tempts who and there is no tip-off till conditional slippage fills up the attic with towering bottoms of wood. Tails some uncut of the lesser cata. Catattattattatappallakkazappatata. Wooden teeth sings of wooden cutouts and ragged flesh and blood flimflam and other gilded lilies craft windows of winter horn toggled tight up against the flipchart you and the buried prattler has an arch intended to debunk the. Tree taller than the one who came to across our mound and found out otherwise the hard way inch. In we mean. Inn a place where you walk into the wall of and out and through.

Gaining confidence.

TWELFTH CHORUS:

Loggia niche niddering O ringlet fancy and the twelve who tan tan cannot can open air to find water's edge and bent wood steam. To belief care's cart seeks highest place for the images. Gun talls and. Gathering erp hop tails. [An OTHER: Not of course cats.] Glittering hop erp tails read to wicker wicca and sleepless go lame. O lama lamest life out agrigentum north to starflow. The asinine. Bulls. Pails of what. In between the utterance. Gadding. Hapless with long hair curving round restlessness hey hey into another's nest.

THIRTEENTH CHORUS:

Not to be deliberate a swan type as tailless as an er cat. Type and toe to head to button can must to prayer ribbon off to thereafter's snow. Hairpin land o danger to thereafter's snow. Hairpin danger to dogs by cat fatal pride of the wold of shelf woe elf. Indignant and slipped. Too. Whatever gathers up steam beneath inaugurate frog. Tail of you know fordidden chopchop. Heheheh. Inauguration template a mystic medallion. Message go and bees. The basket of dynasty worship finds a golf club till Monday is is wiped and erased above the broken ankle spavined joint inflamed tendon repurfle recall remember and forget.

ANSWERER increasingly dubious.

CHORUS FOURTEEN:

So—

ANSWERER:

Wait Wait. Wait. Er,

A choral pause of please to not disturb our circles and the strident ANSWERER is abashed and becomes er docile er.

CHORUS FOURTEEN:

So the leaf-strewn place is a hammer on place to be saying in the cause of what hello and snake offer to the mighty dog ramp. And not cat. Go and just choose all the times as she comes to worst and be an egg. For the pedal gives to in a lawn of place masking between high school and low high hip to hop bop and low bop bop bop and casual intersect till day comes down from the tree there high up photo synthetic and during which no is canoptic jars full of the dead ends of recollected diameters and cat tails. And chopped off chails of chats. All nuthatch and smoke eyed as dust the hand truck pitches up smoky leaves by the auditorium in the way we did an if for sake of what. Tails. What why why what. An imperturbable brong eternally topped in black felt.

Another macrurous pause of the catastastatistical kind. This is a crisis.

ANSWERER:

I repeat: I am here to give voice to that catastasis of tail you la la all of you have caused to chop the tails off of. Er.
Pfaff.

ENFORCER:

Too late.

ANSWERER:

Say that again la la.

ENFORCER:

Too late.

ANSWERER:

See that axe?

ENFORCER:

Return and we will consider a political act on the matter of all possible cats. What about the axe?

ANSWERER:

I am unafraid of the axis of all axes. As for cats too late is too late because er of an imperturbable brong eternally topped in black felt er they have got free. What you said is not what you and them there have done in the factual er. They have got free. Too late as I am beyond the fear place.

———

ENFORCER:

Return. A chorus must speak with one foot otherhow how in what wise can she do the whole damn chorus with one darn voice? By Zaa. By Almanac. By what the wind does when he walks on something with large and wet feet. By what creaks past all unknowing on Crazy Day.

ANSWERER:

Too late.

ENFORCER:

See this axe.

ANSWERER:

Too late.

ENFORCER:

See this axe?

CHORUS: *(imperturbably bronged)*

Groaning and cursing it is it is a day crazy to understand off the will of in the tree basket shadow so some chair is full of black ink. How could we fall so in love with such a cataclysm as you and o one so stipulated by a doubt of universal and random catastrophe and universal cat bye-bye departure? Thou thou stippled thing thou ethically er o stippled creature.

A stippled pause. The ANSWERER *makes to depart.*

The ENFORCER *blocks her way.*

ENFORCER:

Ball's in your* court. *Lap.*

ANSWERER:

Ball's in your court, buster.

The axe is raised; the axe is swung; the chail is topped off.

Pause. Silence. Pause.

Proudly, the ANSWERER *picks up and cradles the severed tail, and slowly continues her journey across the world and off.*

The ANSWERER *is now the* ANSWEARER.

Silence.

Pause.

Silence.

Quietly, the CHORUS *sings the following:*

We all had the black cat
We all had the black cat
But now all we can do
We have a good drink o
We have a good drink o
And kill one another
All on account
That damn black cat.

Quietly, the ENFORCER *sings the following:*

O here I am a wreck
What the heck . . . And
Less of an enforcer
Than ever I guess.

End of scene.

SCENE ≳ : CATECHESIS CATATASTICAL

After the chopping, the ANSWEARER *goes off to the deep wood. Unknown to her, a thousand cats have followed and secretly assembled in the cattails nearby as a new* CHORUS. *She arrives after many days lonely and tired and full of dread. She pauses to sing a song:*

> I sleep and am swept past the door
> I sleep, am swept to the door
> By the tree and am like
> To go dreadful.
> And am like to go
> And am like to go
> And am like to go
> And am like to go
> All dreadful.

Two enormous, fake ears appear in the gloaming. These belong to a a a mysterious HARE. *A shock of recognition, then the shock of not.*

Silence.

Silence.

Pause.

It is unclear to both what is the best way to respond. So they take some time to think this over.

They consider the sky the lake the road the world; they consider a strange vibration from beyond the cattails.

Pause.

Silence.

Silence.

A little scene transpires involving an inaudible squabble between the AN-SWEARER*'s two hands. A squabble over a leaf and a pebble. Suddenly:*

HARE:

Perhaps you wonder why. Well. In a former life I was a sandwich man trapped in low and vulgar sandwich boards. Sandwich boards without a message. Skip it. Never mind the reason. Even before that I was, er, or suffered a translation into, er. Well I was forced by circumstances I am unwilling to divulge to er leave my ancestral homeland, Catatonia, and seek my fortune elsewhere. So I began, like you, to travel. I like travel. Travel broadens the mind, whatever that is that is. Er. Skip it. Well the long and short of it is. You see.

I was arrested, you see, at the airport, all on account of that damn little switchblade knife. You don't know me, I don't know you, so we can speak frankly. I had made the mistake of forgetting to recall that my little knife was not in my checked luggage but in my hand luggage, which I innocently intended to bring aboard the airplane. I had also checked my sandwich boards of course. What a fool I am. Especially in these hard times here you imagine a terrorist under every hat.

A black hat scuttles across the face of the whole world—a very suspicious little black hat.

I have lived many lives, none of them quite what I imagine a life to be. I often wonder, Is my understanding only blindness to my own lack of understanding?

Both consider the implication of this thought.

It often seems so to me. But I am straying from the cat, er, point of my tale.

In the old days I would spend long, long periods of time looking at the moon. I was bigger then, much bigger, and it took me quite a long time to get up from my favorite mud wallow and lumber slowly along to the next. I like to live in swamps and watch the pretty birds, especially the small silvery ones, the ones shaped like bullets. Whizz bangs, I think they were called. Their song reminded me, I suppose, of a time even before that when I had been attached to something else, some dumb and friendly creature lowing softly to her mate through a swamp full of bromeliads and cycads and giant dragonflies the size of paper plates but colored in a glittering peacock-tail spray of iridescent metallica, yes. But I've always liked to follow people about. Oh, I hear something.

Silence. The sound of not much.

Did you hear something? Something off there in the woods?

Oh, I like to follow parades and processions and the retinues and funeral corteges of the rich and powerful because is that not the most beautiful thing they do?

I like the reverse side of coins, the one without a patriotic face on it to disfigure the gleaming metal disc with a low purpose. I like the bottoms of streams and pools, and I like to look for all the lost things that lie there unclaimed: little silvery rings and scissors and ivory combs and hair clips and medallions and keys and toys and toys and all the lost things one cried over losing as a child.

I like to follow close behind; I like to join and attach myself to another; I have great interest in those who have run away in confusion and have suffered defeat and humiliation. I like to gradually disappear, like that smoke over there in the reeds near the rising moon. Hush,

A hush happens . . .

Did I hear the crack of a twig? I did, I think.

When I fly I always sit in the rear of the plane, and that reminds me. Reminds me of my crime. And yes, like you perhaps, I am inclined to fight windmills because I cannot say what it is I really want to say.

Pause.

I like the quiet idea that rides imperceptibly through time and history, like a ripple on a pond.

ANSWEARER:

Er,

HARE:

But my fatal flaw was to pack that damn knife, that exquisite little switchblade knife, in my hand luggage, and not check it with my other possessions as I usually do. I was arrested and suffered all sorts of unpleasant consequences; one thing has led to another; and thus you see me, an internal exile, far from all that know and love me, far from all that I know and love.

ANSWEARER:

—

HARE:

Shall we discuss the matter?

ANSWEARER:

Er, has to do with cats.

Holds out the miserable, severed tail.

HARE:

Cats are bad creatures and cannot be driven by blows.

ANSWEARER:

I cannot be driven by blows. Hot damn.

HARE:

—

ANSWEARER:

Choruses creep me out. Hot damn.

HARE:

Choruses make wide the way with noise, stuff, and. With important stuff and the noise of importance. Cats are silent. You cannot tell where a cat is nor what it is doing.

A twig snaps and far upstage the shadow of pointed ears appears for a moment.

ANSWEARER:

I am tired of all that stuff, stuff, stuff. Hot damn.

HARE:

Let me consider the matter.

He examines very carefully the severed tail.

ANSWEARER:

—

HARE:

—

ANSWEARER:

The tail was not real.

HARE:

Indeed, the tail was not real.

ANSWEARER:

Hot damn er.

Puzzlement of the universal kind.

But the tail was symbolical of another tail, and that tail was real.

HARE:

Is then the symbol the same as the thing symbolized?

ANSWEARER:

Erk.

HARE:

That is what you are saying. You are saying the symbol and the thing are the same.

The ANSWEARER *looks forlornly at her fallen tail.*

HARE:

In many places, like North America, the answer is yea.

In Zmerca yes we all must sling ze djo;
but no one can guess where dem djo must go.

Do you know what you have done?

ANSWEARER:

Hot damn. I have made a promulgation and public pandemocatacratic PROCLAMATION governing the TOTAL and RANDOM departure of cats. Hot damn.

Suddenly, the thousand cats pour out from hiding and form their own chorus.

FIFTEENTH CHORUS:

Singular as put to touch the up to as with a bar of Siamese battle. Torn gap and sub creak to a vow singular as a star below and high. Go to went and be not below the hedges. Roaming where till lies and what matters is the fur. That Yea surely them er chails be not topped. First hunch often to battle the snow and be new of gone dump. My and his way whether to kiss that other shoe as if a hat of truth. Disregard the first look you withdraw and style as multiple union junction riddle time rebate sleeve. O sleeve and wander mouse try till they go ghost. O sleeve and remarkable nut to not biased by the canonical bird hover man tip hat top to clean out bitter closet sayings of the wonder wonder wonder and be not more than no more dried. Upon the riddle and washes washes what cleans yourself and the snow dishes.

SIXTEENTH CHORUS:

O the habit to cause no restlessness among all gift outages in it in she was then and apple girl like a. What still running was that to be water out the sink and tills about the seven between the two others and no easy paradoxical witness. Item: that them chails be not topped. Sweet dream of deer with big white tails. People and hats with valid to till up such as say to each the reed squad hots, nope, stars, in a belly full of had not not experience enough. Turnip. Grasses and a hollow log full of diligence and reward for mortality. It is not old behind the true timothy there. All scratchety. Beat on the hollow wall dividers cannot be down till a taste call all certainty in a busted gut of ingles. So they sow they sew they do a heartbeat away from laughter. Too till the moon spill.

SEVENTEENTH CHORUS:

Inventiveness and apples, soft prong of blackness insect daddy to solid for and clicks pot base gone boat chin wisp spelled by by duster and anywhere as horizon. Hot money as too far horizon. Go cartridge as wheel as crookedness and came of grief. Hot damn. Hot damn. Hot damn. Go breach the bunk twisty bee press caring nothing but a matchless piled over and over an oven horizon by wire sensitive to the touch. O say not case horizon on the steeple on the rump on the wrist as a flinch. Horizon without wall without under part and delivery to the big hand horizon tizzy why and ghastly end to the winter in the cold water place. Nest from which a water song can be heard pits again while the street men and see and hear women clutches dogs cats pelicans on foot to to to a nor horizon go cat go go cats go.

ANSWEARER:

Er,

All the CATS *just as suddenly vamoose and are gone.*

ANSWEARER:

Where have all the cats gone?

HARE:

They will return on another night (this one is nearly done), on the turn of a dime, on the twisk of a twisker, on the click of can opener on can. But they will go again if they are not brushed and stroked and allowed freedom to enact all things catly. All things felinear. All things felineckety. All things including the marking of territory by claw and of season by shedding and regrowth of fur.

ANSWEARER:

Hot damn.

Suddenly impatient.

Let's go someplace else to consider what has been done.

Pause.

Silence.

Paws.

They go someplace else to consider what has been done.

Silence.

Paws.

Silence.

They put down their stuff and rest a little and scratch a little and preen themselves.

Hot damn. Cats is catching.

—

HARE:

We might proceed in this vein, with our conversation, if you like. Is the thing the same as the symbol? You, an Answerer who had become an Answearer, will swear upon a stack of bricks the answer is "No."

ANSWEARER:

Yes. Hot damn. Er, no.

HARE:

But I being both a Hare and a Hair of truth will say, "Yes." And "No."

ANSWEARER:

?

HARE:

For all a chorus is is a sleep of the tongue enabling an each to become an all so that the slender strand of hair of the disagreeable answerer may be redescribed as an answearer and public nuisance.

ANSWEARER:

I a nuisance? Hot damn.

HARE:

Stop saying that.

ANSWEARER:

Er,

HARE:

So the sleep of tongue that forces an each to become an all is also the itch of an each to teach the thing to be replaced by an appropriate symbol so that what is symbolized by our speech is the call of the all of certainty.

ANSWEARER:

Er. Could you paraphrase that? All I said was come the dark I would not be driven by blows.

HARE:

Paraphrase misses the point.

Paraphrase imagines the purpose of a repeated action is to get the thing right.

Paraphrase attempts to enforce a certainty where there is none. And hot damn don't I know what can come of that?

ANSWEARER:

—

HARE: *(singing forlornly)*

O here I am a wreck
What the heck . . . And
Less of an enforcer
Than ever I guess.

ANSWEARER:

YOU!

HARE:

Yes, it is true . . . *(singing again)*
Here I am a wreck . . . And
Less of an enforcer
Than ever I was
I guess.

. . . for after I enforced you they enforced me. That is the longtime rule of all choruses. When an each becomes an all, the all becomes an each. An each and a peach of proper enforcement. All this happens in the hop skip jump from symbol to symbol to symbol. It is the invention of tragedy. The ball that was in your court begets the ball that is in mine.

A tragic paws.

Ball's in your court.

It takes the ANSWEARER *some time to consider the matter and unravel the twisky skein of fate.*

—

ANSWEARER:

There is no certainty, saith the Answearer, only members of the chorus who are certain.

HARE:

Hot damn. You got it right.

ANSWEARER:

Well, er. Look at us. We have gone someplace to consider what has been done. And now we have to ask ourselves. Well, er. Just what has been done?

An unparaphraseable pause.

HARE:

Something has been done.

ANSWEARER:

Apparently.

HARE:

Apparently is the parent of reality. And . . .

Freezes.

ANSWEARER:

I don't get it. So. What is the tragedy in all this?

HARE:

The tragedy in all this is that when we fall out of the all, all we are is an each, even if a peach of an each, an each suspended like a kitten by a single slender hair. A hair so slender it can hardly be seen in the air. A hair so slender it is not the same for all. Each of us suspended by a long slender singular hair. So that we are not the same. We were all the same in the chorus. We are not all the same out there, out here in the open air.

(singing softly)

Each hanging in delight and in care.
In the beautiful morning air
By a single strand of hair.

Indeed, it is nearly morning now, and the rosy-fingered dawn begins to be visible.

For I am not a mere enforcer, no, I am far more than that. O can't you guess?* Guess not. I am your own true tail, not that false new one I chopped. I am your own true tail, which in your ascent to self and in your hope of choral splendor, you sadly misplaced at some forgotten rendezvous, at night, by a Ding Dong tree, because you thought it would betray your origins. Yes, you were ashamed of me.

ANSWEARER:

Er,
Erp.

HARE: *(jokingly)*

In Zmerca yes we all must sling ze djo;
but no one can guess where dem djo must go.

(Now serious.)

Don't, don't you remember? When you slept by the tree and were like to go dreadful?

Now BOTH *sing:*

I sleep and am swept past the door
I sleep, am swept to the door
By the tree and am like
To go dreadful.

And am like to go
And am like to go
And am like to go
And am like to go
All dreadful.

Something rises up behind them.

ANSWEARER:

I see the ears of a cat.

HARE:

Wow.

ALL:

Catastrophe. Catastasis. Cataclysm. *(now quite softly)* All things come all things come and are based on the hope apple. Let there be hope apples, hope apples and donuts of every silvery degree. Let there be a dragon of trees and of washing without washcloths bags cats wardrobes bungle things and other things traps and twerps and words and greater words of estuarial conviviality. La la la la la la la. La la la.

The ANSWEARER *arises and prepares to go off.*

ANSWEARER:

Slender I am and slender I must go.

Walks wire to a far far place.

Pause.

Paws.

Silence.

HARE:

Wow.

Blackout. End of play. Almost.

A pause of the almost completely gone.

For before she goeth she returns.

ANSWEARER:

Let me clarify the matter for another chorus that now is hid.

HARE:

Hot damn, er. Canandadadaddaan.* To thee the soap hath to be up to under the killer's garage.

ANSWEARER:

Let me squeak. Squonk er. Speak.

I have decided to go off to become a single strand, for as long as I do go I shall grow slender and slenderer still, and more slender still.

An evilish CHORUS *of eld appears, suspicicilious, bored, and irritated. Found out, they take off their cat masks and make rude remarks to both* ANSWEARER *and her* ANTAGONISTIC HARE. *Crude faces of the illness er of the Democracy. Envy and contempt of the one who is er more both doth and goth at all things catatatatatastical. Deeds and doods both not to mention the.*

ANSWEARER:

Hear me you tail (some uncut) of the lesser cata.

Catattattattatappallakkazappatata!

CHORUS: *(unmasked)*

Catattattattatappallakkazappatata!

All repeat eleven times.

ANSWEARER:

Should you dread to dare and team up to top er chop this skein of a single strand this other shoe shall unto you have did and go drop.

CHORUS *gasps.*

Slowly unties her shoelaces and drops the other er shoe.

Silence.

Pause through which a semi-tractor-trailer.

Silence.

ANSWEARER:

Except me; the she.

Again she goes out this time for real.

HARE:

Wow. Wow.

CHORUS:

Wow. Catattattattatappallakkazappatata! Wow.

All sing a quiet reprise:

We all had the black cat
We all had the black cat
But now all we can do
We have a good drink o
We have a good drink o
And kill one another
All on account
That damn black cat.

End of play.

Speculations: An Essay on the Theater

Man can do everything but make a birdnest.

—BACHELARD

"Understanding" is a vague concept.

—WITTGENSTEIN

Juoksentilisinkohan.

(In Finnish, I think I shall wander about a little without a particular destination.)

When Goethe went to Italy he traveled part of the way in the company of an Italian captain: "As I would often remain silent and pensive and thoughtful, he said to me once: 'What are you thinking about! One ought never to think, thinking ages one! One should never confine oneself to a single thought because he then goes mad: he needs to have a thousand things, a confusion in his head!' "

—ORTEGA Y GASSET

NOTE

This version of "Speculations" is excerpted from a more complete one (albeit still a work in progress) that is available on the author's Web site at http://www.macwellman.com.

The STRUCTURE of a play ought not be viewed as a fixed thing, but as a mutable one.

I mean, the structure of a play conceived of as a moving point:

→→→→→→→→→ • →→→→→→→→→

passing over—or through—time, from inception to end point; so that what it is relation of part to who(o)le (Oh, Mereology!) changes continuously and continually;

changes because space is filled with invisible lines—as *theatron.* (Da Vinci) This is why vertical narrative is possible.

This is why monologue is inherently demonic.

This is why only the wicked walk in circles. (Augustine)

~

Drama takes place in phase-space. The continuum of phase-space is to time as time is to space.

Theatricality takes place, as it were, perpendicular to time, along the phase-space continuum. We do not know what we are doing.

Thus neither theatricality nor drama takes place in time, although of course they do.

Time (clock-time, I mean) is of the essence only in appearance, not in APPARENCE. Time is only apparently an expression of space; the reverse is also true. (Einstein)

Real thinking as well lies outside time, occupies an outside-time, "that eternal moment that medieval philosophy approached in the *nunc stans* of the mystic." (Arendt)

~

All plots are not stories. All stories are not plots.

The ARISTOTELIAN is the story unfolded as plot.

The STRANGE is the story perpendicular to the ARISTOTELIAN, which unfolds in phase-space, not in time, and hence cannot be told in terms of plot.

~

One might also say: theater enacts the great vanishing and perishing; this is correct because theater, being a vanishing and perishing thing, must exist more in the mind than in the world; we love best what has been removed from us.

~

The Already known is the completion of knowable action (AK = KA). Perfection stands to the AK as AK does to the unknown.

Knowing is touching.

Knowing is touching, yes, but the unknown also happens, has ways, forms shapes, and, yes, even the habit, of a certain kind of tenderness.

The perfect is the radiant; she indicates what is beyond, perpendicular to the square of the Already known: a new dimension—that is, the strange.

The strange fills all phase-space perpendicular to the four dimensions of familiar appearance.

If the Strange is what fills Apparence, Charm is what draws us in. Although these two forces operate in tandem, they are not the same. Their work together inaugurates a state of mindfulness wherein drama, considered as an act of theater (not theatre), can both happen and be noted. As such.

So STRANGENESS is what fills Apparence and, thus, is what keeps us there, where we find ourselves. CHARM is what draws us in and, thus, is what is there when nothing else is.

These two forces (Strangeness and Charm) complete and amplify theater beyond the tragic (impossible in our time) and the Comic now mostly a musty relic of obviousness, obvious incongruity, the Already known (perfected) humor of the GEEZER.

The theater of the Already known is Sentimental Melodrama, which is also Geezer Theatre. (Wellman)

~

All theater is nested; no other than nested theater is possible, although a certain species of Performance can be non-nested.

~

Theater may be nested in a time, a practice, or a culture. This is the What About of the theater.

Space within the theater is, as it were, magnetized by the nest, so recognized. And this is the work of both Strangeness and Charm. And the theater—a place for showing, *theatron*—is thereby endowed.

All theater space is thus filled with an infinity of lines—or vectors (Valery on Da Vinci)—which determine the cogency (or lack thereof) of the theatrical Apperception. (Kant)

This Apperception is not an idea or a concept; it is a geometrical solid, of crystalline architecture, and in these pages it will be denominated an "Apparence."

All theater rests on an awareness of Apparence.

Character, plot, division of entities, coming into and going out ofs, and especially the matter of What About—all these too are part of this coming into awareness.

Personality is not character, though the latter may employ the former.

Personality is one of the scatter-effects of Character.

But Character is refined *(duende, yugen)*; personality is not (personality is like the weatherman on local television).

What scatters, occupies; scatter is the enabler of that which fills the Apparence, insofar as it is the enabler of what is, and what is shown, the theatrical.

Thus theatrical space is a hole filled with something else, something much like theater, but different. Of the same color, but of a different hue.

As a process, this process begins, goes for a time—the wiggle—and then stops.

As a practice, this practice is the doing of Apparence, and what is revealed is like the prayer in the heart of the devotee; what is revealed is boundless, which is a perfection beyond all the perfections of the Already known.

~

Apparence is the actor who knows his lines, and therefore faces the abyss of the Already known (the AK is a naturally occurring antimatter) with perfect equipoise and an amiable demeanor. He is in possession of what he knows, and not the other way around—he knows what he does not know; that is, he practices knowing in the sense of a respect. In this matter, we of the audience are what is wanting, and our mindfulness completes the equation. Truth is the innermost.

Theatrical truth looms enormous, although she exists only on a micro scale.

Unlike the world of the AK, the theater is, in this sense, a study in bliss. Apparence must be calm. Otherwise we are in the wrong place—a theatre perhaps.

All other nestings are false. They divulge their origin being phantoms of the will, perverted contemporary personality. The long underwear of personal expression.

Apparence vanishes or, rather, flees into Hoole Space, which lies perpendicular to time.

Apparence can be made to flee into the precinct of Hoole Space, but it cannot be destroyed. No no no.

We admire self-confidence in actors because we are reminded thereby. Egg and dart sequence. Cosmos. Cosmetic. Decoration. A bliss out of which the antitheatrical world would tumble us, buck naked, as a mere foundling babe.

—

into the vast and cryptic wilderness of Theatre.

Theater is not theatre; he is other than that, a condition of radiants.

If we are lucky we awaken in a HOOLE. Hoole's hole. Where the howl is taken up.

The howl is inaudible to us, the contemporary, being nested approximately in a region of folly, of acoustic shadow; but being wildy the HOWL is a true howl, indeed. Never forget this fact; for this fact is the only fact, and sets all supposes on their noses. (Frost)

Apparence knows the front door can only be approached by the back door. Thus all true actors approach the front door by the back. This is what they do however they talk of the matter. Indeed, if they talk of the matter, they commit an error of redundancy, and are likely to be pricked on the thumb by a thorn. Thus compromised they yell and they yelp. They yelp for help.

A yell is like a yelp, but it is not like a howl. Yelps are beyond help, howls are not. (Ginsberg)

The crie of the yelp can never be stanched; can never be stanched because it is not nested.

He must remain a bogey in the realm of the Already known. A mere motive—.

So: scatter is the flow of intelligence through a visible space.

Scatter both reveals and conceals.

Scatter reveals the theatrical topos with a mathematical precision, albeit along the continuum of phase-space, which is called the M Continuum (M as in Malarkey), and which lies perpendicular to the line of experience, that likewise corresponds to the most commonly held conception of time.

Scatter conceals the theatrical as well; becomes a felt presence, the enabler of what is termed the "uncanny." This presence is a kind of theatrical presence in the absence of what is not, not nested in the Aristotelian, the theater of plot.

Scatter shows us only the outlines, as a kind of event, but also as a species of presence. But as we do not know what it is, we do not know what to do about the matter.

This not knowing about the matter is intrinsic and inescapable. This outcome of the fact of Apparence cannot and must not be resisted.

Plebeian theater (theatre) is a theatrical resistance to, and against, apparence, in the name of appearance.

A question is framed.

A question is raised.

(A question is ignored.)

. . .

Plebeian theatre cannot conceive of any question so framed, so raised. The theatre of our time is, for the most part, a theater of question begging; plebeian theatre is a theatre of the Already known.

The AK knows where it is going, and why.

The AK is not subject to scatter. The plebeian eye sees only what has been before.

This theatre, theatre qua theatre, is tautology.

Theatre qua theatre imagines the world is there merely to be mirrored; there is no prink in her pronk. Theatre qua theatre knows nothing of the What You Will of theater. Theater qua theater.

That is because the What You Will of theater will always go another way; go another way, as though she were a small, dangerous creature, chittering and snarling. Perhaps venomous.

This creature, Black-Tufted Malabar X, knows the world is a terrible, terrible place and wills a compact between special instance and wild time. This creature, this X, glories in the splendor of apparence (and indifference), and keeps her weapons—her dreadful things—her weapons in perfect working order and in crack shape. All in her dreadful box.

The proposition I do not know what I am doing while in the act of doing I do not know who I am or what is not tautology; this proposition reveals an exchange of charm for strangeness. A supersession of apperception by the force of the square of what lies off; off there, and is radiant (and is the Radiant); the radiance of apparence that is perpendicular to the most conventional frame of reference that comes to mind.

Hoole Space is the space of howling.

Structure is that part of the play conceived of as the Already known. Therefore Structure is that part of the play that is like some other play, usually one that is thought to be better or is so deemed (by someone eminent in such matters).

The question of Hoole Space is related to the ontology of theatrical holes, but because of the intension of theatrical airlessness is in effect equivalent to the square of the latter extended at a perpendicular from the familiar.

All such questions are complications of what is called conventional structure.

Conventional structure is a redundancy in fact.

Conventional structure is a redundancy, in fact, since if it were not conventional, there would still be structure present.

There is always structure present.

Structure reveals her plan and purpose as a fractal, at infinite depths.

Thus, in the world of appearance, the structure of the play is that part of the Already known that resembles some other play—as has already been suggested—presumably a better one.

Structure proceeds through historical time on the principle of nested copies, each one slightly more faded than the rest.

Structure exists in the phase-space of fallen time as a cycle of fade.

In the realm of psychology this process is the evolution of what is truly felt to what is not; from an authentic form of sincerity to sentimentality; from true, unmediated feeling to the emotion that is generated as display, in the service of some ulterior motive, or most commonly of What Will Pay the Rent (WWPR).

The gradual conclusion of the whole matter (to paraphrase T. E. Hulme) is that, too often, the language of theatre puts things in a stereotypical form.

That the speciousness of so-called Structure is not at all obvious is one of the effects of Scatter, scatter considered both as charm and as the strange.

We feel things in the prickle on the nape of the neck just as we realize, or are coming to an apperception of the folly of all conventional structures.

All such structures fall down in their folly.

What is, is left standing; standing there in the here and now.
A tear appears.

(A tear as in air; not a tear as in ear.)

A tear appears and it is:

A

↘

↘

such that a gap, or discontinuity, appear

? B

in the continuum.

This we understand or do not understand according to our separate natures.

The thing before us is what is radiant, therefore, in the space of the theater.

We are peripheral to, to appearance.

We are central to the apparence, as it enfolds us in Hoole Space.

All problems are problems of perception.
(All other disturbances are Facts of Life, and hence not problems. Problems capable, in principle at least, of a solution.)

A theater is, thus, a space delimited, a small world for showing and beholding what is shown.

Theater takes place in the world of showing, not in the mind. The mindfulness of theater takes place in this showing. When this showing tips over into the realm of plausible psychological journalism (the Already known), a tear is not enacted, and we are stuck in the world of theatre—a geezerly outcome.

Theater also takes place in the mind, in the order of beholding and apperception. Theater does not take place on stage, because the small world of the stage (so often) becomes a mere pandemonium of fart jokes, hasbeens in fright wigs, fat men and tubas, the whole conboberation of showbiz, a thing to appall anyone with a mind to be appalled.

Still, things happen somewhere theatrically, as we all know what we are talking about in this regard.

—

None of these remarks are unfoldable in the normal three dimensions perceptible to the geezer with his clock dream of totality and social conditioning, and the doing of sixes upon sevens. Rather, these remarks are like the six additional dimensions of Calabi-Yau Space, which remain for most purposes folded up. (Greene)

Folded up like the hidden parts of the sleeping cat.
Because the hidden parts of the sleeping cat are hidden does not mean that the hidden parts are not there.

It is sometimes extremely important to keep things SIMPLE.

Now, therefore, we have observed that all parts of the thing called structure fall down in folly. They do this because unlike the hidden parts of the cat, they appear to be there but they are not.

Structure in this sense is what is not-there; but remains an abstraction, a kind of boilerplate (or theoretical template), a rule of thumb, almost, contrived to comfort the person who does not like theater but is unaware of the fact and being totally clueless is altogether innocent of the folded-up dimensions of the theater (that is, apparence and the scatter-effect of strangeness and charm); and therefore reacts only to the horrifying conboberation of the theatre, a place alien to all other human states. Inevitably, a place full of the very self-assured men and women all talking at the top of their voices.

The point of imagining theater, and the entire experience of being within one, is meaningful precisely in order to avoid the deafening experience of maniacal hubbub described above.

Theat(re) consists of maniacal hubbub more or less successfully disguised.

Theater, properly reconceived and reimagined, presents itself as an apparence, offers an experience close to that of architectural presence. An apperception, out of time (clock-time, at least).

But there might be another kind of time, a time we might call "Wild Time."

We will not consider Wild Time at this moment because we do not know how.

Furthermore, the structure of a play, and I am not referring to structure in the sense of the Already known, is not always the same.

The structure of a play depends on where you are in it.

This should be obvious—your experience of an experience depends on where you are in the experience of experiencing it.

This may seem like madness, but upon further reflection we see that it is not.

We experience theater moment to moment.

That is the only way we experience anything, and it is certainly how we experience a play or what have you in the theater.

Now one of these moments may resemble a point thus:

■

but this moment is not simply a point since if it were a mere point, it would remain a mere figment: a basic and irreducible simplicity at odds with any notion of architecture and of a space to be filled (architecturally, intellectually, emotionally).

But the phase-space of the moment extends perpendicularly to the arrow of clock-time; in clock-time the moment is not extended but remains curled up like the six dimensions of Calabi-Yau Space, like the hidden parts of the sleeping cat.

A point is like the black hole that has no hair: it is irreducible. (Witten)

A moment possesses hair and is therefore like the hidden parts of the sleeping cat.

~

In all this a key concept is multidimensionality; if theater is not to be the crested idiot of theatre, we must think of theater as a multidimensional art form, as architecture, as sculpture (Sculpture and architecture are one [Gaudier-Brzeska]); theater as extension not expression (mere personality).

Of Gaudier-Brzeska: "... his stillness seemed an action." (Pound)

Character and moment and action are one; what is proposed by one is accomplished by another.

Character and moment and action are, in this sense, interchangeable; only each affects a not-knowing of the fact in order to maximize each his and her inmost nature, hue, reflectivity. Each of these elements is like the tilted tile, a tessera, the smallest element of a mosaic.

The purpose of theater in this regard is to oppose thought to thought, with ideas as tesserae, so as to generate more thoughts. Apperception. Epiphany. Thoughts and more of them, a profusion of epiphanies in the order of their appearance—as apparence—in the small world of theater.

Theater is not a means; it is an end in itself. Like truth and democracy. Theat(re) regards the art only as a means, either toward a preestablished and implicit moralism (as in much of the current and faddish British work), or to the end of a set of preconditioned responses; each the opposite side of the coin of the Already known (Geezer theatre, that is, showbiz).

In theater, in a world of lines running perpendicular to clock-time, we have a dialectic of perceptions; perceptions, connections to apperception; apparence.

Apparence, a profusion of tilted surfaces, the momentary, tilted, on a slant.

Theater is alive with surprises, as the GOOSE discovered when she fell down the wrong hole, the Hole of Hoole, Hoole's Hole, a Ho(o)le, and was devoured by small, fierce creatures with wicked claws.

We, being human, want to know why we are doing a thing while we are in the throes of doing it. This want is our disgrace and also our nobility, since without it, we would only be fit for throwing away like trash, like the "abominable branch" that Jonathan Edwards wrote of that so reminded him of himself on a bad day.

Our disgrace because stupid, doomed to frustration, as pointless as gilding the lily.

If the poor GOOSE had not confused Hoole Space with holes in general (and with the ho(o)le of her sad end in particular), she would never have come to be so awfully eaten.

—

But, but always there remains the question of what is nested in what.

For one kind of time may be cunningly nested in another, curled up so we are not aware of her presence.

For time is wriggly.

For time possesseth a definitive attitude.

For time likes to hide, like the Black-Tufted Malabar Xs, small fierce creatures who live in the Hole of Hoole.

For time likes to hide because sometimes time likes to work in secret.

Sometimes time does not wish to hide, but that fact is neither here nor there.

For time likes to hide because she becomes bored with space; there is such a lot of space and most of it mediocre and even an abomination (like the branch).

Space gets very worked up in the stupid pleasures of being three-dimensional.

Time frowns on all this.

Time frowns on all this and sends a wiggly warning.

Time knows the parable of the inchworm. Space does not.

Time could have told (King) Lear a thing or two and would have said something timely obviously timely. Like what the fool saith, what Time says possesseth ins and outs.

For time understands these ins and outs, ins and outs that run in all directions perpendicular to the square of clock-time and so are like the coiled-up dimensions of Calabi-Yau Space and like the hidden parts of the sleeping cat.

(Because when I talk about "time" I am talking about Wild Time.)

Time knows everything. Time knows this and that.

Time knows everything worth knowing, including the fact that Fred's tomato head is made of cloth. Even Fred does not know this fact (apperception).

Fred does not know this, but time does.

Fred, being a Christmas tree ornament, is afflicted with wooden-hair syndrome and hence is stupid.

Time knows fiddle from faddle.

Time knows shadow from hole.

Time knows dust from love and was not ever fooled by either. (Quevado)

Time knows only the wicked walk in circles.

Time knows how to hold the moth wing without touching it too hard.

For time knows touching is knowing.

For time kowtows to no knowing such as the mob knows.

The democracy of objects is a call to action for time's disciples.

For time can indeed tell the difference between Jonathan Edwards and any old abominable branch.

Time can; can Jonathan Edwards? No, he cannot.

This is how theater works. Time and space move slowly and silently, but the animosity between is of an unimaginable intensity.

Profusion devours one, then the other.

In the small space of a theater we call this instantiation theater. This is what we call it because that is what it is called.

When a thing possesses a name, it only makes sense to use that name.

Time speaks very slowly, so as not to be misunderstood, but speaks with an incredible softness.

We don't hear any part of this saying unless we are a saint, a person illuminated by a god. Unless we are in the presence of what happens in the theater.

Space thinks, Something something something.
Time thinks, This will kill that.

2. Due

Repression likes to hide (perpendicular to the square of the Already known).

Why this is I do not know; perhaps it is because things are not just thrown, they are yanked. (Heidegger)

Yank is to throw as charm is to strange.

The matter of this matter constitutes the ins and outs of appearance.

What glides there but is of an unseeable dimension.

Repression likes to hide because once it is found out it may no longer repress.

What kind of repression would that be?

Worse yet, without repression what kind of theater would there be? (There would be no theater at all, only theatre. More precisely, a theatre of the begged question.)

Repression does not smile upon the begged question, because the begged question has no poop in his pizzle, no prink to her pronk.

Repression, thus, is a crested idiot and so must don a mask and fearsome hat.

Repression can see around corners.

Repression is like Newton's Pression: Light cannot be pression, for then wee should see in the night as wel or better than in the day.

Repression works on a bias, by principle of slant and carom.

When you think you have figured out repression, Repression goes elsewhere and you too become the crested idiot.

(We all become the crested idiot.)

The crested idiot's response is a source of comedy because he does not know he does not know he does not know behind which door stands the beautiful girl and which the tiger; no, no, no; but nevertheless he thinks he knows.

The fool.

All people suppose, in such a situation, that either they know they know what the outcome is or or or or at least by what procedure the correct outcome may be arrived at.

Repression knows the crested idiot (all of us) will never guess.

Repression does not have to travel far; there are so many places to hide.

Where? you say. Ha, says repression.

What is repressed, for instance, in Shakespeare is not repressed for us, so that we have only an indistinct idea of what these plays are about. Fearful aboutness. *Lear* and *Hamlet* and *The Tempest* are for us end points of a historical narration that is, so to speak, already known. Shakespeare did not know this, nor did he even know he was Shakespeare. Our productions of his plays are mainly cases of the question begged and beating the dead horse. We miss the apparence of his plays because they are no longer strange. They possess charm in the way an inoffensive person does. These plays represent a threat to no one, which is why the rich and powerful love to see them produced. Love to see them produced in productions where the lily is so gilded it, too, falls down in folly. Shakespeare's lily, that is. We look away in horror and say to ourselves, mayhap is this theater? If this is what theater is, what have I done with my life that, that I am here and not somewhere else where this is not happening? No apparence, only appearance.

For the moment has been embalmed like the archaic bug in the amber of the classic. This is all there is. Left, that is.

Repression is still in the vicinity, only not on stage. Guess where?

Repression is still there, but no one no one no one can say where.

Repression, thus, beholds us in such and such a context, as though we all (each and every one) were merely a vast collection of crested idiots. A sea of smug, complacent, crested idiots from a faded portrait of the olden times; olden times when people possessed not only no clue, but also no poop in her pizzle or prink in his pronk.

The joke on us is, therefore, the joke of being yanked.

Repression has postantedated this removal so that the joke is on us. Surely the joke is on us. Certainly the joke is not on Shakespeare.

(We value Shakespeare for moments, not plots. Who can remember Shakespeare's plots?)

Plot—

Moment.

Situation **~**

A situation is like a nested moment, a moment that serves the same function as plot, only it is extended VERTICALLY in phase-space and not horizontally, as time. A situation is, therefore, charged with strangeness and charm, which is to say, a situation is a moment that has become aware of his own apparence.

~

If theater is repression, how do we maximize it?

If the yanked is to the thrown as charm is to strangeness, how are we to enact a theater that is theater truly? A theater cognizant of repression?

We must always look, as it were, where we are not supposed to. This is nearly impossible in a culture such as ours, so much in lockstep with the Already known.

We must yank ourselves out of all contexts that are determined by the Already known. A prime example of this kind of context is the context of representation.

Yanked representation reveals the thrownness of our lives. (Heidegger) Desperate, bored, irritated, and disconnected lives for the most part. Lives of terror quietened and habitual cluelessness.

The most powerful of all the tribes of the clueless are the Crested idiots (Bierce), and these hate the theater with a terrible fervor, especially when they are themselves employed in the enterprise, parasitical to the structure of theater, as is frequently the case.

(This raises the question of the Already Knowingness of theater's nest-shitters [Big Frank's little old men, Monsoors X and Y, His High Disappointedness, and on and on—they are so many and their voices are as the whispers of the crumpled Playbills of Eld] about which more later.

The dedicated nest-shitter is a remarkable djinn of opinionatedness.)

Repressions of the Already known are not true repressions; they give true repression a bad name. Usually they comprise blocks, bottlenecks, and donut- and torus-shaped acts of censorship. The clueless use repression (in this denuded sense) in the theater (theatre, really) to guide the unwilling to an already known and foregone conclusion.

This is the purpose of all moralistic theatre and British theatre in particular.

Where would we be without the excrementally hued, modular sets that creak and groan, that sprawl about in a sad parody of ingenuity? Where would we be without the British to remind us of the class system (as if we colonial blockheads had no idea of such a thing)? Where would we be without the moral milling machine that is Shaw Churchill Bond and poor Sarah Kane?

Jaws reducing all substance and all matters of interest to pulverized pulp. Grit and dust. Flour Moralized.

Flour for the better class of moral bread. Bread of the better class of nearly everything.

Faugh.

(Are not Brecht and Shaw the same? Only: the German possessing the typical angularity and excellence of the German; the Englishman possessing the rondure and excellence of the English.)

Before this vast moralistic spectacle we stand confused and have not a clue how to behave (that we have not a clue to behave is also the presumption of the TRULY clueless, who typically regard themselves as the modestly mindful elect, and quite distinct from all others in this respect—a myopia of the Already known).

The better class of British theatre is most perturbed by the thought that people can do quite nicely without the class system. The class system is, in this regard, like the (poorly understood) Right to bear arms for many Americans. A holy document, albeit one writ upon intellectual water. If people do not understand the necessity for embracing the class system, they are probably hopeless colonials and monkeys just out of the tree and protofascist scum or something even worse: low class by breeding and conviction. This is a fundamental bulwark of the plebeian temperament: contempt for what is (presumed to be) beneath.

Poor poor Sarah Kane is the last integer in the mechanistic sequence: the case of the iron jaws of the Already known cracking, breaking, and destroying herself because of a palpable absence of grist (for the moral mill). All the vast waste of the immoral Already known has been used up, so where do we go where do we go where do we go (and what do we do)?

As with the moral mastodon of prehistory we come to grief because of a superfluity of tusk. (McLaughlin)

~

This kind of yankedness cannot easily be remedied because of the solemnity of her followers. Britannias's cultural loyalists view the world through a slit in a steel turret, and the outrage they feel is genuine, if ultimately pointless (and clueless).

(Stoppard, Hare, Frayn, all the same.)

(Howard Barker, N. F. Simpson, Louise Page, and the greatest of the Wilsons—Snoo—! Not the same.)

Because one must pay attention not only to what the saying says, but what the saying does.

Because perhaps the purpose of all this moral outrage is precisely to reinforce the class system, and to reintroduce the same in those regions where it has fallen down in folly.

Repression knows there is something fishy about moralism.

~

For the moralism of the theat(re), despite the showbiz glitter, remains moralism—self-righteous and tiresome. One can easily make the argument that it is immoral as well.

Immoral moralism equals imperialism.

All willed things turn; the more intense the willfulness, the more startling the turn.

Why do we need to tell other people what to do?

AND are they doing what they are doing badly or do we disapprove of them because they look funny and act strange?

Theater can deal with these problems better than theatre can because in the truest sense theater has not made up her mind.

Theatre sucker-punches us with the fist of the foregone conclusion.

For the moralism of the theatre has nothing to do with the moral teachings of Christ, Confucius, and Buddha; has nothing to do with the mystery of grace and forgiveness, and transcendence. These things are ineffable; they have no purposefulness, are not tendentious as theatre moralisms are.

If moralism would put on the mask of mockery, the world would be a better place, and American theat(re) might punch a hole though the painted masque to discover the world of apparence (as Orton and Pinter did). This it will never do.

The moralism of the theatre cannot give in to hilarity or mockery, because if it did all attention would pass from moralizing agent to the moralized object (signified hideous other), and even to the moral principle itself, which might not be able to bear scrutiny, "to bear the weight of thought." (Washburn)

Moralism says, Thought object thought object
 thought object.
Mockery and Hilarity say, This will kill that.

Indeed, the theatre of moralism can be described, in this context, as the theatre of the misplaced repression (another version of the Already known).

The theatre of moralism supposes he knows the secret to the Problem of the Mouse and the Three Hats. This is mistaken. No one can tell where the mouse will be, and not even the three hats know. This is the quantum Law of the theater: you cannot know the velocity of the mouse (or of the three hats) and at the same time pinpoint the mouse's precise location (or that of the three hats). The mouse is wriggly and obeys no laws but those of M Theory. Unless you whack the mouse with a hammer, in which case the mouse falls out of apparence (but not appearance).

We feel the effects of scatter; scatter prickles the nape of the neck; moralism prickles not the nape of the anything and makes us wonder why bother why bother why bother why?

Punt.

The only resemblance between scatter and moralism is that both fill the architectural space of the stage.

The moralism of the kind we know in the Western lands leads by the straight-arrow road of improvement to the concrete abutments of Geezer theater. (Wellman)

. . .

Now what exactedally is M Theory?

M Theory is the mother of all theories and is shaped like a house.

Other theories, each and every one, are nested in M Theory in the sense that they all live there.

When one theory gets tired of another theory, he simply gets up and goes out the door; there are many things worth looking at in the world that is out of the door, just sitting there doing nothing (STDN).

Doing nothing is also a kind of theater.

Doing nothing is a kind of theater in the sense that when you are doing nothing you are still doing something.

Theater is a fractal phenomenon.

Theater is a fractal, in the sense that when you take all the drama out of the architectural enclosure of a place you have not removed anything. Certainly not the drama.

You have not removed the drama because drama in the truest sense is everywhere and nowhere. This is the strangest thing a person can know, but it is true.

Drama is likewise a species of repression, and therefore likes to hide. Drama exists for herself alone sub specie aeternitatis.

Theatre says, Showbiz showbiz showbiz.
Drama says, This will kill that.

In other words, if a person in a play is being dramatic (which is to say melodramatic, at least in the context of Anglo American theatre); and say you do not like this Being Dramatic, as it is heavy-handed, obvious, and overdetermined; and say you decide to take this person out and shoot him and happily do so; and say you go and take this dead person and stuff him down the hole the poor GOSLING mistook for Hoole Space and so fell down in folly and was eaten alive by small chattering creatures of the tribe of the Berkeley Silver-Tipped Fennec. And so forth. And anyhow, the Dramatic Person has been removed, and peace and quiet have apparently returned but only apparently because unlike apparence what is apparently the case is only an appearance and often thus a case of the unwarranted assumption. The audience notices that although the Big Person of Drama has been removed, the total amount of drama per se—drama qua drama—remains the same. Only one does not know exactedally where it is; only you do know it is there because the space of the theater is full of strangeness and charm: apparence. Because there is now very little going on does not mean there is nothing going on. Because if your mind and senses have not been numbed and dampened down by continual din of the theatricality of appearance, hooting and holleration, and all the other forms of extensive manifold conboberation—you will begin to feel the prickle of the uncanny as one of the remaining actors does a nothing-something with her great toe (the left one) within the house of her shoe, one of a pair of pretty red pumps.

~

You notice this occurrence as though it were the eruption in 1815 of Mount Tambora. Everyone else notices this moment also, for it is a true moment.

All the people who are present notice this moment because.

Because the moment extends perpendicularly to the square of clock-time; a question is raised and our mindfulness completes the equation.

There is the same amount of drama in the room as there was before.

There is the same amount, but this same amount of drama differs in that whatever it is, she is not of the Already known.

Drama in this sense is not, therefore, something the play makes happens as something the play allows to happen. This is the secret of plays that is largely unknown in our time.

We imagine we are for the most part agents of our destiny, foolish people; but the reason we are able to imagine only this is that we are for the most part instruments of a destiny that, like Wild Time and repression and nature, likes to hide. And like drama.

We cannot flush the drama from the bushes like a sudden detonation of quail.

With our peevish willfulness, we cannot understand how things happen on their own.

The amount of drama in a place is the same, and when the amount of drama in a place changes it is because the architecture of the place has somehow undergone transformation. World works wonder, the old ones say. This transformation may be the result of our doing or not. But transformation can never be solely the result of our willing because we cannot will apparence, only appearance.

Therefore, theater is a fractal phenomenon. Sitting there doing nothing.

△

So we have the instance of Sitting There Doing Nothing (STDN) as the instantiation of a kind of theater unfamiliar to many. It is a phenomenon quite familiar in everyone's life, but unexpected (strange) in the theater where because we have plunked down our dollar we expect something, er, anything to happen.

But anything is not necessarily something.
STDN is baffling to WWPR.

Wanting something, er, anything to happen is the religion of Anglo American theatre. Re-ligio: linking back. Since the something or anything we (they) want to happen is usually an instance of something that has happened before in a more or less PERFECTED fashion, that is, the Already known.

This equation constitutes the Tooth to Tail Ratio of the American theatre; Tooth to Tail Ratio (TTR) is important because he allows us (them) to determine What Will Pay the Rent (WWPR).

However, what happens on stage can never be Perfect, because the TTR is never an exact one; slippage occurs.

The slippage between Tooth and Tail in the TTR is the semeiotic of theater (and theatre), and the valence of these is subject to the "Law of Errors." (Peirce)

An Apperception of errors is only possible because all things pertaining to apparence exist on a perpendicular to the straight arrow of clock-time (Geezer); and to the square of the square of all things geezerly.

The Geezer falls down in folly like Thales the philosopher, but unlike Thales, whose mind was on other matters, the mind of Geezer is on WWPR and stamping out other people's bad thoughts and on religion and the task of re-ligio, namely, linking back to what was is was in order that the obvious be protected by the Already known from whatever exists out there, in the mists and wilds of Wild Time and Hoole Space; whatever it is that sits there (really), there in the center and knows and presumably ate up the poor poor GOOSE. Fell down in folly. Fell down in Hoole's Hole, poor goose.

Geezer goes to the front of the house of M Theory, the mother of all theories, and knocks on the door; repression slinks away heh-hehing to herself and lurks by the back door; Geezer goes all the way round to the back door and knocks, and repression retraces her steps to the front door, quite pleased with herself; Geezer not to be outdone goes round once again by the front door and knocks once more on the carefully locked screen door. Open the door, says Geezer, attention must be paid.

Attention must be paid to Shaw and Brecht (the same fellow) and Horton Foote. Attention must be paid to J. B. Priestly and Athol Fugard. Egad, Arthur Miller, cet imbecile (Ionescu).

Geezer says, Poobah poobah poobah.
Repression, snarkily stabbing flies with her pushpin, says, this will kill that.

The re-ligio fails and falls down in folly because of a faintness of heart.

The re-ligio fails because time is wriggly.

Fails because time too likes to hide.

Fails because apparence is a profusion of tilted surfaces and would not change her nature for a wilderness of monkeys. (Stoker)

Fails because character and moment are one.

Fails because the structure of a play depends on where you are in it.

Fails because a tear (or rip) appears in the continuum.

Fails because we are peripheral to apparence.

Fails because conventional structure is a redundancy.

Fails because theat(re) involves only the most humdrum tautology;

fails because scatter both reveals and conceals;

fails because if we are lucky we awaken in Hoole (or some other wonderful) Space where the howl is taken up;

fails because all theatre rests upon an understanding of apparence, whether we understand the words or not;

fails because charm draws us in;

fails because strangeness fills all space perpendicular to the square of the square of the geezerly;

fails because the unknown is to the Already known as perfection is to the merely plausible;

fails because knowing is touching;

fails because not all stories are plots;
fails because

fails because neither theatricality nor drama takes place in time;

fails because time (but not Wild Time) is of the essence only in appearance, not in apparence;

fails because drama takes place in phase-space;

fails because theater enacts the great vanishing and perishing; because theater being a vanishing and perishing thing must perforce exist more in the mind than in the world; and what we love best has been removed from us.

~

~

(Here the manuscript breaks off, apparently torn with great violence.

The remaining pages, crumpled and wadded, were discovered in the nest of certain, evilish Emerald-hued Macaws, deep within the central regions of impenetrable, forest wilderness at Brooklyn College.)

. . . thus, sub specie aeternitatis, all theatrical presentation involves the enactment of pleasure. This is why theater is worth hating. However, the we who hates theater is not so different from the we who loves. This is true for the obvious reason that one person's X is another's Y. For each is precisely an each one before we are gathered up into an all.

This is the political problem posed by C. S. Peirce: that is, the question whether people really have anything at all in common, considered as the most practical and drastic question, in regard to every possible "political constitution of which we have it in our power to influence."

The apparatus we behold before us, the things presented that constitute the earth and heavens, considered as a machine; all these are the theatrical dream (masculine); opposing are the ramifications of theater considered as reverie (feminine); this is how Bachelard conceived the matter.

The dream is mute, and oddly inexpressive in his own terms; the reverie by contrast offers a proliferation of hints and glimpses (the *epinoia* of Pagels), hues, half-thoughts, suggestions, images, tastes, and sounds, all suggestive of some further half-imagined rapture. The play of the mind considered as the heart and soul's ramificatrix.

(Play considered as a perfection, perhaps negligible, but a perfection nevertheless.)

Likewise, this gathering of each one into a common all is the perfection. Such a gathering is not often considered a species of pleasure, but one it surely is. All our prejudices and social habits confirm this fact. This fact is nowhere more evident than in the theater, which is why tyrants, blockheads, bigots of all kinds, and haters of the common people also hate the theater.

Problem is, they are not so very different from those who love.

In this context, the problem with theat(re) is that it presents the dream as though it were reverie. Because theatre's dream does not trust the reverie, that is, the signifier's capacity to stop time with unlikely trains of thought, images, and wisps of association (and not merely the shibboleths of psychologism), theatre herself is stopped. Or, rather, theater is stopped by theatre. Stopped to no good end, but that of a doctrinal moralism.

This is this; that is that; and never are the twain to meet.

~

For it is apparent that if one does not know what pleasure is, the situation is hopeless. One cannot explain pleasure to one who is lacking in that department, because.

Because.

Because what constitutes the rule of pleasure (misrule in the opinion of some, many even among those under the thrall of the Already known) is an apparence. The availability to pleasure considered as a basic characterological given. Not a psychological given, but a characterological given.

Sheep and goats.

Theater is therefore a pleasure. Theater is therefore a pleasure knowable to the Happy Few for whom access to the pleasurable is not a problem, is not a question of shoulds and oughts.

Because for theater one thing is as good as another, and this is the source of all comedy. Because for theater one thing is not the same as, and cannot never replace, another thing. And this is the source of all tragedy. Each of these masks, each of these faces, is wise, is wisdom incarnate. Because neither buys into the notion of what the Already known thinks is already known. Tautology.

Theater does know that there are already enough tautologies in the world without adding another.

—

Rules. Misrules and the like. These determine what is doable in the theater. As well as what is fetching.

In the theater language can do so much much more than simply advance plot (despite what the better class of crested idiot, c.f. Monsoor Z, supposes). And this doing is not only fetching, she is deeply theatrical.

In any event, storytelling is at its best a wayward and bean-stalking art. Storytelling knows that resistance to plot is as much a part of telling a story as plot. The man who awaits us in the middle of the forest always recedes as we approach. But the crested idiots of the Times are always unaware of this. This is why they are of the Times merely, and have thereby lost their nature.

~~

Theater is a crystal.

The faces of the crystal are related each to each in a way fundamentally different from that of all points on the surface of the sphere to the point that is the center of the sphere.

These faces are planes. Planes of a crystal. The improbable faces of a moving point. The point of the present,

∮

Remember,

as it moves through whatever it moves through,

that point is composed of faces,

faces that stand at similar angle, each to each; faces that move through whatever it is they move through with unequal rapidity and slowness, each to each, prolonging and shortening.

Theat(re) is a sphere.

The surface of that sphere, therefore, is the question begging, theatrically speaking, of the center.

The points on the surface form the collective point of the point of the center.

The sphere is therefore around (and about) the point of the center. They are its point and therefore constitute the belief system of the point of the center.

Belief, noun.
Spiritual marketing.

Strong belief, phrase current (circa 2002). Pro-active hard sell.

This is the theatre of our time, a theatre that is completely round and therefore surrounds a central point with an infinite array of radii—radii that constitute individually and collectively an aboutness.

(While theatre is a sphere, theater is a crystal; hence, the faces of that crystal are not merely about one another. Their relationship is more complex.)

Aboutness is the solid geometry of the theatre.

Aboutness is the rotten issue of our time, a time hopeless and beyond (literally) belief.

Aboutness is the ghastly offspring of Solemnity got upon Caution.

Aboutness is the ghastly by-product of Geezer theater.

Aboutness is what is left when apparence has been driven out.

Aboutness is what is left when Repression has fled and disappeared into the teacup's crack.

Aboutness is the war of appearance against apparence.

Aboutness refuses to see the world as it is, a broken place.

Aboutness rejects the frangible and opaque because these are not part of the Already known.

Aboutness rejects landscape as a point of view.

Aboutness does not understand what it means to be always ahead or always behind of what is going on.

Aboutness does not bother with what is going on because what is going on is not part of WWPR.

Aboutness does not understand the landscape (of theater) as an instance of architecture revealed.

Aboutness does not understand motion in one place.

Aboutness does not understand anything that is in and for itself.

Aboutness cannot (and will not—on principle) understand the statement that resemblance is not the business of painting (and theater).

Aboutness certainly does not understand the statement (also by Stein) that in composition one thing is as important as another.

Lastly, aboutness cannot comprehend that things happen as they happen.

Finally, aboutness cannot imagine that in the aristocracy of feelings patience is the most revered.

Aboutness is the Beach Ball Bob of theatrical yes-men. A witless and semi-unemployable drama-turgo.

Aboutness is a ball that bounces, but bounces flatly.

The outs of Aboutness, indeed, lack any sort of convincing bounce.

BB Bob exemplifies the chronic case of public speaking in our time: A brilliant idea,

Which occurred to him once upon a time, and has been a standing marvel (for and to himself) ever since then. (C. Wright)

BBB does not understand why Darwin said, Never use the words "higher" and "lower";

or, in the discourse of Jesus with Nicodemus in the gospel of John: The wind bloweth where it listeth, and thou hearest the sound whereof but canst not tell whence it cometh, and whither it goeth, and how it scattereth with strangeness and charm; so is everyone that is born of the spirit.

~

For the story that we are telling in the theater when we are telling anything is a story, perforce, that must go on forever or not at all.

The story is either a point or a line:
A . ; or a — .

The story goes on without us when we stop telling it.

The Master Illusion Builder says, This is enough for now, so I shall get off of the running board for now.

Story says, I abide, I shall abide, I shall always abide.

Just as pleasure, often, has nothing to do with (mere clock-) time.

Real time, Wild Time, goes on being whatever it is, and we know only what it does.

~~

Plot is a way of managing story.

Plot and story become synonymous in the theatre of the Already known.

Plots view the theatrical manifold with suspicion.

Plots view theatrical hullabaloo with suspicion.

Plot views the world darkly.

Plot views the world darkly because the world is a wicked awful mess. Plot would like to tidy things up a bit.

Plot would like to sort things according to which goes with which, and put everything in a proper box.

Plots are against nature.

Plots are against nature, which is why story is always trying to wriggle out of plot's grasp like an impatient young cat (Ah yi! Ah yi!), unwilling to be held a moment longer.

Theatrical hullabaloo says,
Lapsus calami,
Lapsus linguae,
Lardy Dardy.

Story says, And then, and then, and then.
Plot says, Too much here, too little there, too much
there, too little here.

Plot believes in lines, not in the dramatic poetry of what pools or puddles, certainly not in the apocalyptic drama of the merest point.

These latter phenomena are intrinsically unpindownable and therefore have no cash value, and hence no reality at all in the metaphysical system of WWPR.

Indeed, theatrical moments are, aesthetically considered, perfect examples of the Intensive Manifold. Their manifoldyness is intrinsic, and therefore they cannot be taken apart.

A theatrical point may be thought of as a musical chord.

A theatrical point happens all at once.

Because a theatrical point happens all at once does not mean it perforce must be a simple point.

A point, oh let us be let us be less geometrical and call it a moment, yes, a theatrical moment! May be complex, nay, must be complex, if only because it is inextricable.

All moments are theatrical because all moments possess strangeness and charm and stand perpendicular to the square of the square of the obvious and to the casque of appearance.

Indeed, experience as we all know it, insofar as we are capable of experiencing anything, is a story that is composed of a set of moments.

A story composed of a set of moments may possess a plot, or not.

A story composed of a set of moments may prefer her moments scattered about in an irregular jumble. (Allard)

The jumble may be jumbled but the story remains in some senses tellable, even if such a telling appeals not to the better class of theatre Geezer.

We all know stories, real theatrical stories, stories that we love and savor and cackle at, and do our best not to reveal to the theater Geezers among us because they would say no no no, this cannot be denominated a story proper cannot be so denominated because such and such constitutes an instance of the heresy of motion in one place. (Kierkegaard, as before noted)

Because no one goes to the theater to hear a plot enacted.

Some may say this is so, but it is not so, and the people in question do not know what they are doing in so saying.

Unless they are Geezers and under the malign influence of all things geezerly.

In the theater we respond to moments we like and do not respond to those that are not our cup of tea.

This is the way we respond because it is the only sensible way to respond if we are responding truly and not merely Going Through the Motions of seeming to respond when in fact we are not in any sense having a real experience worthy the name.

The function of the better class of theater critic is to protect society from the momentary. But perhaps

True responses are, as before stated, apocalyptic and therefore constitute a threat.

Going Through the Motions sees threats in every direction, and rightly so, because space is filled with infinite lines of force.

And these lines of force are composed of theatrical moments, each one of which is liable at any moment to pop.

To become an apocalyptic event for someone who was not paying much attention to the plot of the pay because.

Because the whole thing was boring.

Because.

Because moments happen. A true story is an aggregate of distinct moments, moments, a moment-cluster in the variorum of spaciotemporal continuum. As members of an aggregate they may be plotted, even if they may not always be said to conform to a predictable plot sequence.

Because things pop, are always popping.

Because the crucial point is that these moments may be plotted only after the fact, though they may be plotted before they have, so to speak, occurred, as an appearance.

Because plots are one of the means of the Already known to give plausibility to the appearance of something that has happened, while attempting to maintain hegemony over each instance of what happens (good luck!).

Because What Happens is subject to the phenomenon of scatter, and if a crested idiot is not lucky he and she is liable to fall down into the hole of Ho(o)ole Space with the poor COW.

Because apparence consists of an aggregate of points that can be plotted only after they have happened and have become, so to speak, an array.

The beauty of apparence is that it always follows from what has happened or is doing so before our very eyes.

Because what happens takes place in a field wherein vectors, or lines of force, may be drawn, in an infinite array from each point to every other point.

And it is perhaps this that Kierkegaard meant by motion in one place.

Because that which is lovely, is lovely only when it appears. (Edwards)

Because moments are just that, momentary.

Because all moments are epiphanies in the wilderness of Wild Time. Because it is precisely in the momentary that we are able to overcome the hegemony of the Already known.

Because moments considered an epiphany take us away from all that.

Because much of what constitutes the Already known is just gassing, is just four miles of hot air. (Wittgenstein)

Because all this is so is why doing theater in our time has become such a tricky proposition. Repression has found new and unlikely places to establish her nest.

All this is obvious to the Happy Few who have rejected the lure of being about, and who do their best to remain a bit skeptical concerning the matter of what we think we know.

Because the Already known may consist of what we think we know but in a more deeply considered sense do not possess even the foggiest notion of.

Someone has to be the Emperor of Ice Cream.

Someone has to be the FOOL.

Someone has to be totally CLUELESS concerning the nature of the nonsense he and she are uttering.

—

For one person's nonsense is another's truth, but there is no measure in this regard; however, this does not prevent both from being nonsensical. It may simply be the case that both persons are correct only in their low regard of the other. This is the kind of time (circa 2002) we would seem to inhabit.

If in current politics (if one can call it that) the liberal's nonsense is called opinion, then surely the conservative's is conviction. Whatever. In all this, nonsense multiplies both opinion and conviction; because anything that divaricates splits along the fault lines of the crystal, reveals himself as dimorphic. We fear the dimorphic because we are reminded that ironies abound not merely in our lapsi calami and lapsi linguini but in the fabric of reality itself.

Perhaps the fundamental irony, more disturbing than any other to the mob mentality of antitheatrical MAN, is that the world was not prepared for our well-being, that she does not exist for us. Nor does he take much cognizance of us, because. Because we are boring.

If we were able to be aware of the true nature of our boring world, and of the elasticity of time, we would be wise. If only the FOOL would persist in his folly. (Blake)

(To be boring is to be lost in noise, emotional static.)

Because the realism of the New age arises from the noise of the Old one.

Because the theatrical arises out of what despises the theatrical. The reason does not matter.

The reason why does not matter because the reason always comes along after the fact.

Once it occurs, the fact does not need to be justified because the meaning of the moment is a theatrical event.

Because the display of the moment is an instance of something that happens.

Because a moment constitutes an epiphany, as before stated, and cannot be understood under the rubrics of the Already known.

Moments are epiphanies.

An epiphany is drama, nothing else.

The drama is an epiphany, something opens up.

Something shows itself.

Something is revealed that was there all along.

Something rears back and yells, Ah yi! Ah yi!

So, the drama of our lives, unlike the drama of the Already known, does not run on rails.

Drama is discursive and recursive. She says to herself, I wonder if I should wander around a little without a particular sense of destination (*Juoksentilisinkohan* in the Finnish language).

Because we are boring, half the time, we would not recognize drama if it came up to us and bit us on the ass.

Because the proverbial bite on the ass is also a kind of ceremony.

Ceremony emerges from the corpse of theatre (and other forms of the Already known) as a kind of alien chest-burster. (Vide Wellman, elsewhere)

Ceremonies go on a little, then stop, or peter out.

Ceremonies are moments illuminated by other ceremonies, ceremonies that happened once and are likewise happening now, in some possible world. (Lewis)

(This has nothing to do with the knowing of the Already known, since like theater ceremony is a practice based on doing, not a belief system of knowingness described throughout these pages.)

Ceremony is the nonlinear optic on the moment.

Ceremony is the basic form of the theatrical.

Obvious ceremony, the investiture of nobles, prelates, and politicians, for examples, is what passes for ceremony in the public mind. But no no no, these stand to the more basic and certainly more wonderful ceremonies as dog food does to dog.

For live ceremony feeds on dead ceremony.

We are barely aware of the ceremonious nature of our lives.

(Were we slightly more aware of these ceremonies we would fall down in the hole of Ho(o)le Space, like poor poor Wiplala. Were we very much more aware of these we would perhaps no longer be people per se. People qua people. We would be something else. Angles and T squares. Protractors and other divine beings.)

The doing of ceremonies thus constitutes the main fact and purpose of our lives.

Lives considered as interim solutions—those of the solitary individual, and those of lives considered socially, as members of a community, presumably with some important things in common.

One must write presumably because one kind of very special ceremony is the hoax.

Indeed, no true ceremony is entirely free of hoax; for if it were totally free of hoax, he could not, given the theatrical and apocalyptic nature of moments, be a true a true ceremony.

All things theatrical are dimorphic, are two-fold. In a sense, they are duplicitous.

For Two is the number of the Adversary (and all things adversarial).

There is nothing wrong with this.

Indeed, the hoax is good to think upon if one would seek to be rooted in a world that cares not a whit for our purposes.

Ceremony saves us from our own wrath, and the odium of our good intentions.

Ceremonies save us, period.

We good people go to the grave with our dear dead friend—but we do not climb down the ladder into the ground. No, we do not do not do not do this. Why not?

We do not do this because.

We do not do this because to do so would be an attempt to grasp the unknowable by means of the Already known.

To do so would violate the rules of the ceremony.

Rules simple. Rules unwritten. Rules unwritable. Rules unspeakable even.

The one who is now dead and gone has undergone a momentous translation, has become a character in a different play. A different play from the one we know.

And we come back to the point of all this nonsense.

Ceremony is the point of all this, as the point of the arrow moves through time:

→→→→→→→→→ • →→→→→→→→→

For plays exist in time
(not quite).

End

(Finally, concerning the wHo(o)le question of taking up the howl, I propose to remain silent.)

Mac Wellman is Donald I. Fine Professor of Playwriting at Brooklyn College. He has received three Obie awards, most recently in 2003 for lifetime achievement. He is the coeditor, with Young Jean Lee, of *New Downtown Now: An Anthology of New Theater from Downtown New York* (Minnesota, 2006).

Helen Shaw is a New York theater critic whose work appears in the *New York Times* and *Time Out New York*.